N

MW01137475

WEST PUBLISHING COMPANY

P.O. Box 3526

St. Paul, Minnesota 55165

October, 1980

Administrative Law and Process, 1972, 336 pages, by Ernest Gellhorn, Professor of Law, University of Virginia.

Agency-Partnership, 1977, 364 pages, by Roscoe T. Steffen, Late Professor of Law, University of Chicago.

Antitrust Law and Economics, 2nd Ed., (February, 1981), approx. 430 pages, by Ernest Gellhorn, Professor of Law, University of Virginia.

Church-State Relations—Law of, (November 1980), about 315 pages, by Leonard F. Manning, Professor of Law, Fordham University.

Civil Procedure, 1979, 271 pages, by Mary Kay Kane, Professor of Law, University of California, Hastings College of the Law.

Civil Rights, 1978, 279 pages, by Norman Vieira, Professor of Law, University of Idaho.

Commercial Paper, 2nd Ed., 1975, 361 pages, by Charles M. Weber, Professor of Business Law, University of Arizona.

Conflicts, 3rd Ed., 1974, 432 pages, by Albert A. Ehrenzweig, Late Professor of Law, University of California, Berkeley.

Constitutional Analysis, 1979, 388 pages, by Jerre S. Williams, former Professor of Law, University of Texas.

I

NUTSHELL SERIES

Constitutional Power—Federal and State, 1974, 411 pages, by David E. Engdahl, former Professor of Law, University of Denver.

Consumer Law, 2nd Ed., (February, 1981), approx. 400 pages, by David G. Epstein, Dean and Professor of Law, University of Arkansas and Steve H. Nickles, Professor of Law, University of Arkansas.

Contracts, 1975, 307 pages, by Gordon D. Schaber, Dean and Professor of Law, McGeorge School of Law and Claude D. Rohwer, Professor of Law, McGeorge School of Law.

Corporations—Law of, 1980, approx. 365 pages, by Robert W. Hamilton, Professor of Law, University of Texas.

Corrections and Prisoners' Rights—Law of, 1976, 353 pages, by Sheldon Krantz, Professor of Law, Boston University.

Criminal Law, 1975, 302 pages, by Arnold H. Loewy, Professor of Law, University of North Carolina.

Criminal Procedure—Constitutional Limitations, 3rd Ed., 1980, approx. 425 pages, by Jerold H. Israel, Professor of Law, University of Michigan and Wayne LaFave, Professor of Law, University of Illinois.

Debtor-Creditor Law, 2nd Ed., 1980, 324 pages, by David G. Epstein, Dean and Professor of Law, University of Arkansas.

Employment Discrimination—Federal Law of, 2nd Ed., (November 1980), about 365 pages, by Mack A. Player, Professor of Law, University of Georgia.

Estate Planning—Introduction to, 2nd Ed., 1978, 378 pages, by Robert J. Lynn, Professor of Law, Ohio State University.

NUTSHELL SERIES

NUTSHELL SERIES

Judicial Process, 1980, 292 pages, by William L. Reynolds, Professor of Law, University of Maryland.

Jurisdiction, 4th Ed., 1980, 232 pages, by Albert A. Ehrenzweig, Late Professor of Law, University of California, Berkeley, David W. Louisell, Late Professor of Law, University of California, Berkeley and Geoffrey C. Hazard, Jr., Professor of Law, Yale Law School.

Juvenile Courts, 2nd Ed., 1977, 275 pages, by Sanford J. Fox, Professor of Law, Boston College.

Labor Arbitration Law and Practice, 1979, 358 pages, by Dennis R. Nolan, Professor of Law, University of South Carolina.

Labor Law, 1979, 403 pages, by Douglas L. Leslie, Professor of Law, University of Virginia.

Land Use, 1978, 316 pages, by Robert R. Wright, Professor of Law, University of Arkansas, Little Rock and Susan Webber, Professor of Law, University of Arkansas, Little Rock.

Landlord and Tenant Law, 1979, 319 pages, by David S. Hill, Professor of Law, University of Colorado.

Law Study and Law Examinations—Introduction to, 1971, 389 pages, by Stanley V. Kinyon, Late Professor of Law, University of Minnesota.

Legal Interviewing and Counseling, 1976, 353 pages, by Thomas L. Shaffer, Professor of Law, Washington and Lee University.

Legal Research, 3rd Ed., 1978, 415 pages, by Morris L. Cohen, Professor of Law and Law Librarian, Harvard University.

NUTSHELL SERIES

Real Estate Finance, 1979, 292 pages, by Jon W. Bruce, Professor of Law, Stetson University.

Real Property, 1975, 425 pages, by Roger H. Bernhardt, Professor of Law, Golden Gate University.

Remedies, 1977, 364 pages, by John F. O'Connell, Professor of Law, Western State University College of Law.

Res Judicata, 1976, 310 pages, by Robert C. Casad, Professor of Law, University of Kansas.

Sales, 2nd Ed., (January, 1981), approx. 350 pages, by John M. Stockton, Professor of Business Law, Wharton School of Finance and Commerce, University of Pennsylvania.

Secured Transactions, 1976, 377 pages, by Henry J. Bailey, Professor of Law, Willamette University.

Securities Regulation, 1978, 300 pages, by David L. Ratner, Professor of Law, Cornell University.

Titles—The Calculus of Interests, 1968, 277 pages, by Oval A. Phipps, Late Professor of Law, St. Louis University.

Torts—Injuries to Persons and Property, 1977, 434 pages by Edward J. Kionka, Professor of Law, Southern Illinois University.

Torts—Injuries to Family, Social and Trade Relations, 1979, 350 pages, by Wex S. Malone, Professor of Law Emeritus, Louisiana State University.

Trial Advocacy, 1979, 402 pages, by Paul B. Bergman, Adj. Professor of Law, University of California, Los Angeles.

Trial and Practice Skills, 1978, 346 pages, by Kenney F. Hegland, Professor of Law, University of Arizona.

NUTSHELL SERIES

Uniform Commercial Code, 1975, 507 pages, by Bradford Stone, Professor of Law, Detroit College of Law.

Uniform Probate Code, 1978, 425 pages, by Lawrence H. Averill, Jr., Professor of Law, University of Wyoming.

Welfare Law—Structure and Entitlement, 1979, 455 pages, by Arthur B. LaFrance, Professor of Law, University of Maine.

Wills and Trusts, 1979, 392 pages, by Robert L. Mennell, Professor of Law, Hamline University.

Hornbook Series

and

Basic Legal Texts

of

WEST PUBLISHING COMPANY

P.O. Box 3526

St. Paul, Minnesota 55165

October, 1980

———

HORNBOOKS & BASIC TEXTS

Common Law Pleading, Shipman's Hornbook on, 3rd Ed., 1923, 644 pages, by Henry W. Ballantine, Late Professor of Law, University of California, Berkeley.

Conflict of Laws, Goodrich and Scoles' Hornbook on, 4th Ed., 1964, 483 pages, by Eugene F. Scoles, Professor of Law, University of Oregon.

Constitutional Law, Nowak, Rotunda and Young's Hornbook on, 1978 with 1979 Pocket Part, 974 pages, by John E. Nowak, Professor of Law, University of Illinois, Ronald D. Rotunda, Professor of Law, University of Illinois, and J. Nelson Young, Professor of Law, University of Illinois.

Contracts, Calamari and Perillo's Hornbook on, 2nd Ed., 1977, 878 pages, by John D. Calamari, Professor of Law, Fordham University and Joseph M. Perillo, Professor of Law, Fordham University.

Contracts, Corbin's One Volume Student Ed., 1952, 1224 pages, by Arthur L. Corbin, Late Professor of Law, Yale University.

Contracts, Simpson's Hornbook on, 2nd Ed., 1965, 510 pages, by Laurence P. Simpson, Professor of Law Emeritus, New York University.

Corporate Taxation, Kahn's Hornbook on Basic, 3rd Ed., (November, 1980), approx. 550 pages, by Douglas A. Kahn, Professor of Law, University of Michigan.

Corporations, Henn's Hornbook on, 2nd Ed., 1970, 956 pages, by Harry G. Henn, Professor of Law, Cornell University.

Criminal Law, LaFave and Scott's Hornbook on, 1972, 763 pages, by Wayne R. LaFave, Professor of Law, University of Illinois, and Austin Scott, Jr., Late Professor of Law, University of Colorado.

HORNBOOKS & BASIC TEXTS

Damages, McCormick's Hornbook on, 1935, 811 pages, by Charles T. McCormick, Late Dean and Professor of Law, University of Texas.

Domestic Relations, Clark's Hornbook on, 1968, 754 pages, by Homer H. Clark, Jr., Professor of Law, University of Colorado.

Environmental Law, Rodgers' Hornbook on, 1977, 956 pages, by William H. Rodgers, Jr., Professor of Law, University of Washington.

Equity, McClintock's Hornbook on, 2nd Ed., 1948, 643 pages, by Henry L. McClintock, Late Professor of Law, University of Minnesota.

Estate and Gift Taxes, Lowndes, Kramer and McCord's Hornbook on, 3rd Ed., 1974, 1099 pages, by Charles L. B. Lowndes, Late Professor of Law, Duke University, Robert Kramer, Professor of Law Emeritus, George Washington University, and John H. McCord, Professor of Law, University of Illinois.

Evidence, Lilly's Introduction to, 1978, 486 pages, by Graham C. Lilly, Professor of Law, University of Virginia.

Evidence, McCormick's Hornbook on, 2nd Ed., 1972 with 1978 Pocket Part, 938 pages, General Editor, Edward W. Cleary, Professor of Law Emeritus, Arizona State University.

Federal Courts, Wright's Hornbook on, 3rd Ed., 1976, 818 pages, including Federal Rules Appendix, by Charles Alan Wright, Professor of Law, University of Texas.

Future Interest, Simes' Hornbook on, 2nd Ed., 1966, 355 pages, by Lewis M. Simes, Late Professor of Law, University of Michigan.

HORNBOOKS & BASIC TEXTS

Partnership, Crane and Bromberg's Hornbook on, 1968, 695 pages, by Alan R. Bromberg, Professor of Law, Southern Methodist University.

Property, Boyer's Survey of, 3rd Ed., (January, 1981), approx. 737 pages, by Ralph E. Boyer, Professor of Law, University of Miami.

Real Estate Finance Law, Osborne, Nelson and Whitman's Hornbook on, (successor to Hornbook on Mortgages), 1979, 885 pages, by George E. Osborne, Late Professor of Law, Stanford University, Grant S. Nelson, Professor of Law, University of Missouri, Columbia and Dale A. Whitman, Professor of Law, University of Washington.

Real Property, Burby's Hornbook on, 3rd Ed., 1965, 490 pages, by William E. Burby, Professor of Law Emeritus, University of Southern California.

Real Property, Moynihan's Introduction to, 1962, 254 pages, by Cornelius J. Moynihan, Professor of Law, Suffolk University.

Remedies, Dobbs' Hornbook on, 1973, 1067 pages, by Dan B. Dobbs, Professor of Law, University of Arizona.

Sales, Nordstrom's Hornbook on, 1970, 600 pages, by Robert J. Nordstrom, former Professor of Law, Ohio State University.

Secured Transactions under the U.C.C., Henson's Hornbook on, 2nd Ed., 1979, with 1979 Pocket Part, 504 pages, by Ray D. Henson, Professor of Law, University of California, Hastings College of the Law.

Suretyship, Simpson's Hornbook on, 1950, 569 pages, by Laurence P. Simpson, Professor of Law Emeritus, New York University.

HORNBOOKS & BASIC TEXTS

Torts, Prosser's Hornbook on, 4th Ed., 1971, 1208 pages, by William L. Prosser, Late Dean and Professor of Law, University of California, Berkeley.

Trusts, Bogert's Hornbook on, 5th Ed., 1973, 726 pages, by George G. Bogert, Late Professor of Law, University of Chicago and George T. Bogert, Attorney, Chicago, Illinois.

Urban Planning and Land Development Control, Hagman's Hornbook on, 1971, 706 pages, by Donald G. Hagman, Professor of Law, University of California, Los Angeles.

Uniform Commercial Code, White and Summers' Hornbook on, 2nd Ed., 1980, 1250 pages, by James J. White, Professor of Law, University of Michigan and Robert S. Summers, Professor of Law, Cornell University.

Wills, Atkinson's Hornbook on, 2nd Ed., 1953, 975 pages, by Thomas E. Atkinson, Late Professor of Law, New York University.

Advisory Board

THE LAW OF CHURCH-STATE RELATIONS
IN A NUTSHELL

By

LEONARD F. MANNING

Cameron Professor of Law,
Fordham University

ST. PAUL, MINN.
WEST PUBLISHING CO.
1981

COPYRIGHT © 1981 By WEST PUBLISHING CO.
Printed in the United States of America

Library of Congress Cataloging in Publication Data

Manning, Leonard F   1917–
  The law of church-state relations in a nutshell.

  (Nutshell series)
  Includes indexes.
  1. Religious liberty—United States.
I. Title.
KF4783.Z9M36   342.73'0852   80–22991

ISBN 0-8299-2113-3

To
M.C.M.

*

PREFACE

We are told by Thucydides that Cleomenes, in a fitful wrath, banished from Athens the descendants of the archons who had dishonored the temples of the Acropolis. The wrath of Cleomenes, a Spartan, may well have been contrived to demean the Athenians. But, honest religious convictions have aroused honest rage in even the most religious of leaders. Long before Greek fought Greek for predominance in Peloponnesia, did not Moses, enraged by the Israelites who danced about the golden calf, smash the stone Tablets upon "the spurs of the mountain"? And Moses ordered, in the name of the Lord, that the sons of Levi put to death those of their brothers, their friends and their neighbors who had been guilty of idolatry.

Religious issues seem always to flame emotional fires. So it is with decisions of the United States Supreme Court in that area of our law which has been rather loosely described as "Church and State." Mr. Justice Black wrote with judicious understatement when he said of those decisions, "Probably few opinions of the Court in recent years have attracted more attention or stirred wider debate."

This little volume has not been written to participate in that debate, nor to draw conclusions respecting the historical accuracy or inaccuracy of the Court's decisions. It has a singular, very simple and most unemotional purpose: to state the present position of the United States Supreme Court respecting the Religion Clauses of the First Amendment.

I have, however, some apprehension that the title, "Church and State", might itself be suspect, —and vulnerable to discreet criticism. Neither the word, "church," nor the word, "state," appears in the First Amendment. There is a certain prejudgment implicit in the words themselves. They imply a continuing judicial acceptance of Jefferson's metaphorical "wall of separation between church and state." The caption, "Freedom of Religion," might have been chosen. But, that title, too, suggests a certain predetermination. It rejects out of hand the absolutist concept of separation hardened by a "high and impregnable" wall, and it implies that "separation of church and state" is no more than a means to implement the principle of religious freedom.

A title, though, is a trivial thing. "Church" and "State" are the chosen words of cataloguers, curricula craftsmen, lexicographers and legal scholars, including some who have sat and who sit on the United States Supreme Court—individuals of various faiths or of none at all. Whatever else those words may imply, the title, "Church and State," is taken here as a shorthand substitute for the precise language of the First Amendment's Religion Clauses.

The language itself can carry no predisposition —except that of those who proposed and who ratified the Amendment. The meaning thereof does require the tracking of a doctrinal development through the decisions of the United States Supreme Court. And, it may be idle—as Mr. Justice Jackson once stated respecting the offering of religious instruction in public schools—to pretend that we can find in the First Amendment, or elsewhere in the Constitution, one word to help us decide where the secular ends and the sectarian begins. But Mr. Justice Jackson was surprisingly severe when he concluded that the matter is one "on which we can find no law but our own prepossessions." His stated frustration is understandable, but it would be most presumptuous for anyone, save a Justice of the Court, to suggest that the Court has been possessed by unprincipled prejudices.

So, the language itself is our point of departure in search of the meaning of the First Amendment's Religion Clauses. The venture is undertaken free of all possible personal predilections and free of any shadow of fear that the Court, or any Justice thereof, has at any time suppressed judicial objectivity.

Before scratching the historical surface of the Constitution's Religion Clauses and proceeding into the decisions of the Supreme Court, I must note, with gratitude, the consent of the Editors of the Washington Law Review to the reproduction, with revisions, of modest segments of an article I wrote for their journal, way back in 1964, on the occasion of Mr. Justice Douglas' twenty-fifth anniversary as an Associate Justice of the Supreme Court of the United States. The article is "The Douglas Concept of God in Government," 39 Washington Law Review 47–73 (1964).

In the interest of ease of reading, parallel citations to United States Supreme Court decisions have been omitted. The "star paging" system in both the Supreme Court Reporter and the Lawyers' Edition of Supreme Court Reports enables the reader to locate pertinent cases and passages from Supreme Court decisions by use of the citation to the official U.S. case reports.

L.F.M.

New York, N.Y.
October, 1980

OUTLINE

CHAPTER ONE. THE RELIGION CLAUSES OF THE UNITED STATES CONSTITUTION

CHAPTER TWO. THE ESTABLISHMENT CLAUSE

OUTLINE

CHAPTER THREE. THE FREE EXERCISE CLAUSE

*

TABLE OF CASES

References are to Pages

TABLE OF CASES

TABLE OF CASES

TABLE OF CASES

The Law of
CHURCH – STATE RELATIONS
in a
Nutshell

CHAPTER ONE

THE RELIGION CLAUSES OF THE UNITED STATES CONSTITUTION

§ 1.01 Ratification of the Constitution and of the Bill of Rights

Congress submitted the Constitution to the states on Sept. 28, 1787. The states ratified the Constitution in the following order: Delaware, Dec. 7, 1787; Pennsylvania, Dec. 12, 1787; New Jersey, Dec. 18, 1787; Georgia, Jan. 2, 1788; Connecticut, Jan. 9, 1788; Massachusetts, Feb. 6, 1788; Maryland, April 26, 1788; South Carolina, May 23, 1788; New Hampshire, June 21, 1788; Virginia, June 26, 1788; New York, July 26, 1788; North Carolina, Nov. 21, 1789 and Rhode Island, May 29, 1790.

Massachusetts, New York, Virginia and other states desired that there be a "Bill of Rights" in

the Constitution and it was with the tacit understanding that they would have one that those
states ratified the Constitution. On Sept. 25, 1789,
during the first session of the first Congress, the
first ten amendments (the Bill of Rights) were
proposed. The eleventh state, Virginia, there then
being fourteen states in the union, ratified them
on Dec. 15, 1791.

§ 1.02   The Prohibition of Religious Tests for Public Office

The Constitution, as originally adopted, made no
reference to religion except for the provision in
Art. VI, cl. 3, that "no religious Test shall ever be
required as a Qualification to any Office or public
Trust under the United States."

This clause on its face would seem to be limited
to federal office. And it seemed to be so understood by the ratifying states. Religious tests had
been widespread in the colonies. After independence was achieved, similar tests were written into
the constitutions or statutes of most of the original
states. New York, for example, required a test
oath which rendered Roman Catholics ineligible for
state office. Other states prescribed the profession
of a belief in the Protestant religion. Several demanded only a belief in the Christian religion and
some only a belief in God.

Criticism of religious tests for the holding of any
public office had been heard in the Constitutional

Convention of 1787 and a tide of opposition to those tests gathered force in the last decade of the eighteenth century. But, it was long into the nineteenth century before tests based upon a belief in Protestantism or even Christianity disappeared. It was 1806 before the first Roman Catholic took his seat in the New York State Assembly. North Carolina's test remained until 1835, New Jersey's until 1844, and the swell did not sweep across the narrow shores of New Hampshire, where the principal state offices were restricted to Protestants, until 1877.

Even then there remained in the constitutions of eight states provisions which prescribed, or authorized the legislature to prescribe, an oath or affirmation of a belief in God as a qualification for holding state office. Maryland's constitutional phrasing was typical. It stated that "no religious test ought ever to be required as a qualification for any office of profit or trust in this State, other than a declaration of belief in the existence of God." Not until 1961 was this "declaration of belief," and effectively all state pre-emptions of public office through tests oaths, invalidated. Torcaso v. Watkins, 367 U.S. 488 (1961).

The Maryland test oath was challenged for the first time when Mr. Roy Torcaso had been refused a commission as a notary public only because he would not declare his belief in God. Mr. Justice Black, writing for an unanimous Court, found it "unnecessary to consider appellant's contention that [the test oath proscription of Art. VI, cl. 3] applies to state as well as federal offices." Id. at 489, n. 1. The Maryland oath was invalidated as violative of the Religion Clauses of the First Amendment.

The Court's reasoning has rendered the specific prohibition of Art. VI superfluous. It is in the First Amendment, by its terms made applicable to Congress, and perforce of the Fourteenth Amendment (§ 1.05, infra) made applicable to the states, that we find the complete summation of our Constitutional law as it pertains to the relation of government to religion and of religion to government.

§ 1.03   The Provisions of the First Amendment

"Congress shall make no law respecting an establishment of religion, or prohibiting the free exercise thereof * * *". U.S. Const. amend. I.

In those sixteen words the First Amendment sets forth the Constitution's religious guaranty. It is a simple statement encompassing two compact clauses, the first known as the Establishment Clause, the second as the Free Exercise Clause.

The Establishment Clause was once described by Mr. Justice Rutledge (borrowing James Madison's characterization of Jefferson's Bill for Establishing Religious Freedom) as " 'a Model of technical precision, and perspicuous brevity.' "   Everson v.

Board of Educ., 330 U.S. 1, 31 (1947) (Rutledge, J., dissenting).

We may well be wary of the Rutledge characterization. The "perspicuous brevity" which he admired so much is the end product of an historical obscurity respecting the meaning of the precise words and the original intent of those who proposed and who ratified the First Amendment. In the records of the Constitutional Convention, in Congressional debates, in the history of an era we may find the meaning of other clauses of the Constitution, but in this instance historical soundings are disturbingly discordant. See § 2.01 infra. It is appropriate to note what Chief Justice Marshall wrote a long time ago—albeit respecting another clause in the Constitution, "This provision is made in a constitution intended to endure for ages to come, and, consequently, to be adapted to the various crises of human affairs." McCulloch v. Maryland, 17 U.S. (4 Wheat.) 316, 415 (1819). Certainly then, Mr. Chief Justice Burger's reading of the Religion Clauses, in Walz v. Tax Comm'n, 397 U.S. 664, 668 (1970), adhered to the Marshall philosophy of Constitutional construction and his reading was more perceptive than that of Justice Rutledge.

> The Establishment and Free Exercise Clauses of the First Amendment are not the most precisely drawn portions of the Constitution. The sweep of the absolute prohibitions

in the Religion Clauses may have been calculated; but the purpose was to state an objective, not to write a statute. In attempting to articulate the scope of the two Religion Clauses, the Court's opinions reflect the limitations inherent in formulating general principles on a case-by-case basis. The considerable internal inconsistency in the opinions of the Court derives from what, in retrospect, may have been too sweeping utterances on aspects of these clauses that seemed clear in relation to the particular cases but have limited meaning as general principles.

There are, indeed, "limitations inherent in formulating general principles on a case-by-case basis" but the tests of Establishment (§ 2.02 infra) and the rules of construction respecting the Free Exercise Clause (§ 3.01 infra) have emerged from the Court's decisions with considerable clarity, however much individual convictions or personal philosophies may have divided the Court in the application of those tests. Nor is there, at least in one respect, any lack of clarity in the very first word of the First Amendment, "Congress." It announces that the First Amendment is not applicable to the states. But see § 1.05 infra. Yet, in another respect, it is a cryptic first word. Does it imply that the amendment is not operative to restrict the President and the executive department, to restrict the judiciary?

[6]

§ 1.04 The First Amendment as a Restriction on Presidential and Judicial Powers

Of the ten amendments proposed by Congress in 1789, now our Bill of Rights, only the First mentions Congress. The other nine amendments are phrased in the passive voice without identifying the subject of the restraint—e. g., "* * * the right of the people to keep and bear Arms, shall not be infringed." U.S. Const. amend. II.

The initial version of what now constitutes the first two clauses of the First Amendment was James Madison's proposal to amend Article I, § 9 of the Constitution by adding thereto the clause, "The Civil rights of none shall be abridged on account of religious belief or worship, nor shall any national religion be established * * *." In the course of its journey through the House of Representatives the Madison proposal was, on motion of Fisher Armes, restated in the affirmative and capped with the word "Congress." In that style, with its present wording, it ultimately emerged from the joint House and Senate Committee on Conference in late September, 1789. The records of the First Congress do not disclose, however, any reason for the grammatical restructuring or the reference to Congress. To infer that the amendment was not intended to restrict the executive department or the federal judiciary would be little more than syntactical speculation.

The Court has yet to address the issue directly. But, there is language in a score or more of cases which sweeps both the executive and the judiciary within the First Amendment's restrictions. The sweep is almost unmistakeable insofar as it affects the federal courts. In Watson v. Jones, 80 U.S. (13 Wall.) 679 (1871) the Supreme Court held that federal courts lack the power to resolve church property disputes by a judicial determination of ecclesiastical dogma. *Watson* was, however, a diversity case decided before the First Amendment was made applicable to the states by absorption into the Fourteenth Amendment. Also, it antedated Erie R. R. Co. v. Tompkins, 304 U.S. 64 (1938) and it applied general federal law rather than the state law of the forum in which the suit was brought. The *Watson* Court made no reference to the First Amendment but it did say that it "would lead to the total subversion of * * * religious bodies, if any one aggrieved by one of their decisions could appeal to the secular courts and have them reversed," 80 U.S. (13 Wall.) at 729, and a later Court perceived in the language of *Watson* "a clear constitutional ring." Presbyterian Church v. Mary Elizabeth Blue Hull Memorial Presbyterian Church, 393 U.S. 440, 446 (1969).

The First Amendment has been held to inhibit *state* court review of ecclesiastical decisions. But, the First Amendment is applicable to the states only via the Fourteenth Amendment and the Fourteenth Amendment is addressed not to the state legislature alone but to the "state" in all its governmental functions. In those cases limiting state court adjudication of religious dogma the Supreme Court has, however, consistently written in terms more comprehensive than the precise holding. The Court has repeatedly stated that the First Amendment interdicts "civil courts", thus implying a restriction on all courts, both state and federal. See, e. g., Serbian Eastern Orthodox Diocese v. Milivojevich, 426 U.S. 696 (1976) and cases cited therein. Indeed, it would seem somewhat anomalous to apply the First Amendment to state, but not to the federal, courts.

Kedroff v. St. Nicholas Cathedral, 344 U.S. 94, 116 (1952), also gave Watson v. Jones a Constitutional gloss. "The opinion," wrote Mr. Justice Reed, "radiates * * * a spirit of freedom for religious organizations, an independence from secular control or manipulation * * * ." Does it put an undue stress on an isolated phrase to suggest that "secular control or manipulation" embraces the presidency as well as the courts and Congress? Surely, it does not strain Mr. Justice Black's studied restatement of the first clause of the First Amendment, "The 'establishment of religion' clause * * * means at least this: Neither a state nor the *Federal Government* can set up a church." Everson v. Board of Educ., 330 U.S. at 15 (1947). (Emphasis added). The Black restatement has been regularly reiterated and reaffirmed in subsequent Establishment Clause decisions of the Supreme Court. It is not unreasonable to conclude, even in the absence of a direct holding, that there is an unquestioned judicial consensus, or at least an accepted assumption, that the Religion Clauses of the First Amendment apply to the executive and to the judiciary as well as to the Congress of the United States.

§ 1.05   The First Amendment as a Restriction on the States

Whatever Delphic double meaning we may be required to give to the word, "Congress," to limit presidential and federal judicial powers, it would seem implicit in the term itself that the First Amendment is not applicable to the states. Despite the negative wording of the following nine amendments, and the absence of any reference to Congress therein, it is adequately clear from the annals of the First Congress that no part of the Bill of Rights was intended to impose restrictions upon the states. The Supreme Court so held, reading its conclusion in "the history of the day." The Court stated that it was an expressed fear of abuse of federal power, voiced in "almost every convention by which the constitution was adopted," which inaugurated "[t]hese amendments [as] security against the apprehended encroachments of the general government—not against those of the local governments." Barron v. Baltimore, 32 U.S. (7

Pet.) 243, 250 (1833). Though *Barron* was a Fifth
Amendment holding, Chief Justice Marshall's dictum, embracing the entire Bill of Rights, was repeatedly reaffirmed. See, e. g., Permioli v. First
Municipality, 44 U.S. (3 How.) 589 (1845); Walker
v. Sauvinet, 92 U.S. 90 (1875); Presser v. Illinois,
116 U.S. 252, 265 (1886). *Permioli* specifically held
that the Free Exercise Clause of the First Amendment was inapplicable to the States.

The idea that the Privileges and Immunities
Clause ("No State shall make or enforce any law
which shall abridge the privileges and immunities
of citizens of the United States") of the Fourteenth
Amendment, adopted in 1868, incorporated the Bill
of Rights, and thereby imposed its inhibitions upon
the states, was rejected in 1873. Slaughter-House
Cases, 83 U.S. (16 Wall.) 36, 77-78 (1873). Then,
in 1940 the Court used the Due Process Clause
("nor shall any State deprive any person of life,
liberty or property, without due process of law") of
the Fourteenth Amendment as the vehicle for applying the Free Exercise Clause of the First
Amendment to the states. Cantwell v. Connecticut, 310 U.S. 296 (1940).

In *Cantwell* the Court struck down a Massachusetts licensing statute which, as construed and applied, required a permit to disseminate religious
literature. Thus the Court was concerned with
religious liberty and not with an establishment of

religion. Mr. Justice Roberts, however, wrote of both clauses.

> The fundamental concept of liberty embodied in [the Fourteenth Amendment] embraces the liberties guaranteed by the First Amendment. The First Amendment declares that Congress shall make no law respecting an establishment of religion or prohibiting the free exercise thereof. The Fourteenth Amendment has rendered the legislatures of the states as incompetent as Congress to enact such laws. 310 U.S. at 303.

The absorption of the Free Exercise guarantee by the Fourteenth Amendment's word, "liberty," is understandable. Both pertain to freedom. The logic of Justice Roberts' ipse dixit incorporation of the Establishment Clause is not as persuasive. Religious liberty can co-exist with an established church. There is religious liberty in England, for example. There is also an established church. The Establishment Clause stated a rule regulating the governmental relationship between the states and the Federal government. There were nine established (or state-preferred) churches in the original states. Not until 1833 was the last of these disestablished. It was not "an establishment of religion" which was condemned as were prohibitions or abridgments of the freedoms of religion, of speech, of the press and of assembly. Congress was simply forbidden to take any action at all, either for or against, i. e., "respecting," an establishment of religion. Nonetheless, without further explication, Murdock v. Pennsylvania, 319 U.S. 105, 108 (1943), another Free Exercise case, reaffirmed *Cantwell's* dual incorporation dictum.

Four years later, in Everson v. Board of Education, supra, an Establishment decision, the Court declared—solely on the authority of *Murdock*—that the Establishment Clause applies with equal force to both state and federal governments. *Everson* held, however, that the New Jersey statute, challenged there, did not violate the Establishment Clause. Technically, the *Everson* incorporation principle might, therefore, be considered a dictum. It remained for McCollum v. Board of Educ., 333 U.S. 203 (1948) to apply the Establishment Clause to invalidate a state law. The application, via the Due Process Clause of the Fourteenth Amendment, of both Religion Clauses to the states, has been reaffirmed in a multitude of subsequent cases. See, e. g., Roemer v. Maryland Public Works Bd., 426 U.S. 736 (1976), and decisions cited therein. It is now judicially settled beyond all reasonable doubt.

CHAPTER TWO

THE ESTABLISHMENT CLAUSE

§ 2.01 Historical Considerations—the Original Meaning

"Undoubtedly the Court has the right to make history," Edward Corwin once remarked, "but it does not have the right to *remake* it." Corwin, The Supreme Court as a National School Board, 14 Law & Contemp.Prob. 3, 20 (1949). (Emphasis in original). Professor Corwin was protesting the Establishment Clause rationale of Everson v. Board of Education, supra, and the Court's decision in McCollum v. Board of Educ., supra. In his view of history the Establishment Clause, as applied to Congress, prohibited only *preferential* treatment of any particular religion or any particular sect.

Corwin's conclusion has the support of another distinguished scholar, Justice Joseph Story, who wrote that "[t]he real object of the amendment was * * * to exclude all rivalry among Christian sects, and to prevent any national ecclesiastical establishment which should give to a hierarchy the exclusive patronage of the national government." 2 Story, Commentaries on the Constitution of the United States § 1873 (5th ed. 1833). This "preferential" reading also finds some footing in the historical fact that the Northwest Ordinance, passed by the Continental Congress in 1787, was reenacted two years later by the same First Congress which proposed the First Amendment. As reenacted the Ordinance provided in part, "Religion, morality, and knowledge being necessary to good government and the happiness of mankind, schools and the means of education shall forever be encouraged."

Mr. Justice Black, the author of the *Everson* majority opinion, read his history through a different glass: "The 'establishment of religion' clause * * * means at least this: Neither a state nor the Federal Government * * * can pass laws which aid one religion, *aid all religions*, or prefer one religion over another." 330 U.S. at 15. (Emphasis added). Justice Black focused almost exclusively on the writings of Jefferson and Madison. He recounted their dramatic and successful struggle in the 1785–1786 Virginia legislature to defeat renewal of Virginia's tax levy for support of its established church. He noted that it was in opposition to the Virginia law that Madison wrote his famous Memorial and Remonstrance wherein Madison argued (in Black's rephrasing) that no person, either believer or non-believer, should be taxed to support a religious institution of any kind.

Finally, Justice Black quoted the provision in "Virginia's Bill for Religious Liberty," originally written by Jefferson and enacted by the Virginia Assembly, "No man shall be compelled to frequent

[15]

or support any religious worship, place, or ministry whatsoever * * *." He concluded his history lesson with the sentence, "This Court has previously recognized that the provisions of the First Amendment, in the drafting and adopting of which Madison and Jefferson played such leading roles, had the same objective and were intended to provide the same protection against governmental intrusion on religious liberty as the Virginia statutes." 330 U.S. at 13.

Is this an oversimplification of history, deficient in its exclusion of what transpired in the First Congress? Marshall had noted in Barron v. Baltimore, supra, that the state conventions which ratified the Constitution demanded a federal Bill of Rights. The Bill of Rights is a contemporary of the Constitution. Would it not be appropriate, then, to consider what those conventions desired and intended, and to consider as well the debates in the legislatures of the several states which ratified the First Amendment? These questions have often been asked, but from the answers of apparently competent scholars it is impossible to put together a consensus as to the original meaning of "an establishment of religion." It is as though there has been a scholarly conspiracy to disagree. It is, of course, beyond the compass of a nutshell to evaluate, or even to catalogue, those historical dissertations. It must suffice to note the existence of the controversy and the fact that it has not yet subsided.

Twenty-two years after the *Everson* decision Mr. Justice Harlan wrote:

> [W]e have recently been reminded that the historical purposes of the religious clauses of the First Amendment are significantly more obscure and complex than this Court has heretofore acknowledged. Careful students of the history of the Establishment Clause have found that "it is impossible to give a dogmatic interpretation of the First Amendment, and to state with any accuracy the intention of the men who framed it * * *." Above all, the evidence seems clear that the First Amendment was not intended simply to enact the terms of Madison's Memorial and Remonstrance against Religious Assessments. Flast v. Cohen, 392 U.S. 83, 125-126 (1968) (Harlan, J., dissenting).

In 1970 Chief Justice Burger found other perplexities. Although he too declined the dogmatic, he discerned, as already noted, "considerable internal inconsistency" in the Court's Establishment and Free Exercise opinions. For all of the Court's prior historical dissertations, for him it was sufficient "to note that for the men who wrote the Religion Clauses of the First Amendment the 'establishment' of a religion connoted sponsorship, financial support, and active involvement of the sovereign in religious activity." For him the sole specific dictated by the First Amendment is that "we will not tolerate either governmentally established religion or governmental interference with religion" but short "of those expressly proscribed governmental acts there is room for play in the joints productive of a benevolent neutrality which will permit religious exercise to exist without sponsorship and without interference." Walz v. Tax Comm'n, supra, 397 U.S. at 668–669. But, in 1971 and again in 1976, Justice Brennan espoused the dogmatic. He adhered to his previously asserted view—blessed by him as "one which accords with history and faithfully reflects the understanding of the Founding Fathers"—that "[w]hat the Framers meant to foreclose * * * are those involvements of religious with secular institutions which (a) serve essentially religious activities of religious institutions; (b) employ the organs of government for essentially religious purposes; or (c) use essentially religious means to serve governmental ends, where secular means would suffice." Lemon v. Kurtzman (Lemon I), 403 U.S. 602, 642 (1971) (Brennan, J., concurring); and see, Roemer v. Maryland Public Works Bd., 426 U.S. at 770–772 (Brennan, J., dissenting). The Brennan reading of history would leave "play in the joints" with the Equal Protection Clause where Mr. Justice Holmes had found it. Bain Peanut Co. v. Pinson, 282 U.S. 499, 501 (1931).

The *Everson* Court, it must be noted, did not confine itself to the Jefferson-Madison pre-Constitutional concepts of religious liberty and/or establishment. On Jan. 1, 1802 President Jefferson wrote a letter to the Danbury, Connecticut Baptist Association in which he observed that the Religion Clauses of the First Amendment (not the Establishment Clause alone) were intended to erect "a wall of separation between church and state." What Jefferson wrote was a symbolic way of summarizing the effect of the First Amendment's Religion Clauses. But it was neither a complete statement nor a substitute for the words of the amendment itself. The Court, however, put its judicial imprimatur on Jefferson's metaphor and added that the wall must remain "high and impregnable." 330 U.S. at 16, 18.

The Court's adoption of the Jefferson metaphor as a restatement of the Establishment Clause drew Mr. Justice Reed's curt response, just one year later, "A rule of law should not be drawn from a figure of speech." McCollum v. Board of Educ., 333 U.S. 203, 247 (1948) (Reed, J., dissenting). A scrupulous student might also note that the Court read Jefferson's letter to the Baptist Association slightly out of context. Jefferson's wall was raised in protest against the establishment of a Congregationalist state church in Connecticut, one which continued there until 1818. Jefferson objected to state support of one religion to the exclusion of all other religions.

But, is there anything really wrong with wrapping a rule of law in a figure of speech? Nothing really—if it is used as a fair and accurate shorthand expression of a more complex principle. But, there is something foreboding in a wall particularly when it is built "high and impregnable." It does not make for good neighbors. It suggests hostility between government and religion, an hostility which would be difficult to reconcile with the espousal of "religion and morality" in the Northwest Ordinance which was reenacted in August of 1789, the very month the First Congress was debating the very wording of the Establishment Clause.

The wall metaphor alarmed some religious groups in the United States, particularly Roman Catholics. The diabolical consequences (for religion and the religious, at least) which those groups read into *Everson*'s historical undertones and its firming of the wall of separation proved to be exaggerated. Mr. Justice Black did not, after all, advocate complete and uncompromising separation. He did find a crevice in the wall, large enough to permit Ewing Township to pay the transportation expenses of children attending church-related schools. Other fissures have appeared with the passage of time. Their appearance, and the ultimate crumbling of the wall itself, will be noted in the development of the judicial doctrine for evaluating laws and practices, state and federal, which have been proscribed or permitted as being or not being "an establishment of religion."

§ 2.02   The Evolution of a Judicial Doctrine

(a) The Pre-Everson Jurisprudence

"Our system at the federal and state levels is presently honeycombed" with governmental financing of religious exercises, Mr. Justice Douglas once said.   Engel v. Vitale, 370 U.S. 421, 437 (1962) (Douglas, J., concurring).   But, as he footnoted there and stated elsewhere, Zorach v. Clauson, 343 U.S. 306, 313 (1952), it is not the product of a recent hive.   The bees were busy long, long ago, even in the First Congress which provided for chaplains in both Houses of Congress and in the armed services.   To be sure, as long ago as 1817 Congress subsidized *religious* education among the Indian tribes, a practice which continued until the turn of the century.   Yet, an Establishment issue was never put squarely before the Court until Bradfield v. Roberts, 175 U.S. 291, in 1899.   There, Joseph Bradfield, a citizen and taxpayer of the United States and a resident of the District of Columbia, challenged, as an Establishment of Religion, an appropriation by Congress to Providence Hospital, "a   private   eleemosynary   corporation * * * composed of members of a monastic order or sisterhood of the Roman Catholic Church," pursuant to a contract between the hospital and the Commissioners of the District of Columbia.

Mr. Justice Peckham, for a unanimous court, rejected the Bradfield claim.   He reasoned that the hospital was a corporation, a secular entity, chartered by Congress and it was not transformed into a religious agency merely because its members were Roman Catholic nuns. He added:

> Nor is it material that the hospital may be conducted under the auspices of the Roman Catholic Church. To be conducted under the auspices is to be conducted under the influence or patronage of that church. The meaning of the* allegation is that the church exercises great and perhaps controlling influence over the management of the hospital. It must, however, be managed pursuant to the law of its being. That the influence of any particular church may be powerful over the members of a non-sectarian and secular corporation, incorporated for a certain defined purpose and with clearly stated powers, is surely not sufficient to convert such a corporation into a religious or sectarian body. 175 U.S. at 298.

A religious establishment, then, is not synonymous with "an establishment of religion" and a Congressional grant to the former does not result in the latter, not, at least, where the religious establishment serves the secular purpose of "keeping a hospital in the city of Washington for the care of such sick and invalid persons as may place themselves under the treatment and care of the corporation." 175 U.S. at 299–300.

In Quick Bear v. Leupp, 210 U.S. 50 (1908), decided nine years later, plaintiff and other members
of the Sioux tribe of Indians contested payments
made by the Commissioner of Indian Affairs and
other officers of the United States to the Bureau
of Catholic Indian Missions to provide for the religious education of the Sioux. The Constitutional
issue was not pressed before the court. Chief
Quick Bear had argued only that the appropriation
was contrary to a legislative enactment of Congress. This argument based on the legislated policy of Congress, as well as any Constitutional issue
that might have been raised, was nicely disposed
of by noting that the payments came from "treaty
funds" and "trust funds," monies which belonged
to the Sioux in the first place and, therefore, the
Court concluded, the case did not involve an appropriation of federal funds. The Court observed
that some reference had been made "to the Constitution in respect to this contract with the Bureau of Catholic Indian Missions" and, citing Bradfield v. Roberts, somewhat duplicitously replied, "It
is not contended that it is unconstitutional and it
could not be." 210 U.S. at 81.

Establishment next came before the Court in
Arver v. United States (Selective Draft Law
Cases), 245 U.S. 366 (1917), wherein the draft law's
exemption of ministers and of students in divinity
and theological schools and its grant of non-combat
status to members of religious sects whose tenets

excluded the moral right to engage in war were challenged. The challenge was given curt and summary disposition in a single sentence,

> And we pass without anything but statement the proposition that an establishment of a religion or an interference with the free exercise thereof repugnant to the First Amendment resulted from the exemption clauses of the act to which we at the outset referred, because we think its unsoundness is too apparent to require us to do more. 245 U.S. at 389–390.

Finally, before the advent of *Everson*, in 1930 came Cochran v. Louisiana State Bd. of Educ., 281 U.S. 370. An establishment issue was surely presented. Louisiana had provided secular textbooks, free of charge, to children attending church-related elementary schools. The Court resolved the first amendment issue by simply ignoring it. It found that education, including the secular education provided by church-related schools, served a public purpose and that, therefore, the textbook gratuity did not constitute a taking of taxpayers' property for private interests in derogation of the Fourteenth Amendment's Due Process Clause. While the establishment issue was by-passed in *Cochran* the Court's holding became an ingredient of the majority's ruling in Everson v. Board of Educ.

(b) Everson v. Board of Education

Everson gave us the Court's first explicit exposition of the Establishment Clause. It remains the landmark decision. *Everson* sustained, against an Establishment Clause challenge as well as a *Cochran*-like due process challenge, the right of New Jersey's Ewing Township (which provided bus transportation for public school pupils) to finance bus transportation for children attending parochial schools.

On the due process issue *Everson* turned to *Cochran.* Citing the latter, Justice Black wrote:

> It is much too late to argue that legislation intended to facilitate the opportunity of children to get a secular education serves no public purpose. * * * The same thing is no less true of legislation to reimburse needy parents, or all parents, for payment of the fares of their children so that they can ride in public busses to and from schools rather than run the risk of traffic and other hazards incident to walking or "hitchhiking." * * * Nor does it follow that a law has a private rather than a public purpose because it provides that tax-raised funds will be paid to reimburse individuals on account of money spent by them in a way which furthers a public program. 330 U.S. at 7.

This is the lesson of Bradfield v. Roberts—but with a cavalier, or perhaps intentional, disregard of the potential for religious permeation of secular subjects present in Ewing Township's parochial school, a potential permeation which was obviously absent in Providence Hospital's eleemosynary care of the sick.

Justice Black's evaluation of *Cochran* was carried over, but only inferentially, to his Establishment Clause principle. He wrote:

> [W]e cannot say that the First Amendment prohibits New Jersey from spending tax-raised funds to pay the bus fares of parochial school pupils as a part of a general program under which it pays the fares of pupils attending public and other schools. It is undoubtedly true that children are helped to get to church schools. There is even a possibility that some of the children might not be sent to the church schools if the parents were compelled to pay their children's bus fares out of their own pockets when transportation to a public school would have been paid for by the State. * * * Moreover, state-paid policemen, detailed to protect children going to and from church schools from the very real hazards of traffic, would serve much the same purpose and accomplish much the same result as state provisions intended to guarantee free transportation of a kind which the state deems to be best for the school children's welfare. And parents might refuse to risk their children to the serious danger of traffic accidents going to and from parochial schools, the approaches to which were not protected by policemen. Simi-

larly, parents might be reluctant to permit their children to attend schools which the state had cut off from such general government services as ordinary police and fire protection, connections for sewage disposal, public highways and sidewalks. Of course, cutting off church schools from these services, so separate and so indisputably marked off from the religious function, would make it far more difficult for the schools to operate. But such is obviously not the purpose of the First Amendment. 330 U.S. at 17–18.

At this juncture the *Everson* rationale cried for clarification. If the indirect financial aid to the church-related school, which it sanctioned, be founded on a child-secular-education principle, then other forms of governmental aid to such schools would be permissible, though not required. If it be founded on a child safety principle then bus transportation for children attending parochial schools, commensurate with that provided public school children, might conceivably be required.

Everson told us what Constitutionally could be done in the service of a secular or public purpose. It also told us that which could not be done:

Neither a state nor the Federal Government can set up a church. Neither can pass laws which aid one religion, aid all religions, or prefer one religion over another. Neither can force nor influence a person to go to or to

remain away from church against his will or
force him to profess a belief or disbelief in any
religion. No person can be punished for enter-
taining or professing religious beliefs or dis-
beliefs, for church attendance or non-atten-
dance. No tax in any amount, large or small,
can be levied to support any religious activities
or institutions, whatever they may be called,
or whatever form they may adopt to teach or
practice religion. Neither a state nor the Federal Government can, openly or secretly, participate in the affairs of any religious organizations or groups and *vice versa.* 330 U.S.
at 15–16.

Thus, religion, qua religion, could no more be the
victim of governmental discrimination than it
could be the recipient of its bounty. From this
point of view only a law couched in exclusively
religious terms and serving only an exclusively religious purpose would offend the Establishment
Clause.

(c) The McCollum-Zorach Divergence

The *Everson* rationale was rigidly applied in Mc-
Collum v. Board of Educ. (1948), supra, but relaxed, over Justice Black's dissent, in Zorach v.
Clauson, 343 U.S. 306 (1952). *McCollum* found unconstitutional the in-school "released-time" program adopted in Champaign, Illinois. The "Champaign Plan," which Vashti McCollum (whose son
was a student in a primary grade of the Cham-

paign public school) sought to enjoin, permitted religious instruction to be given by private or outside religion teachers to those children in the public elementary school whose parents so requested. It was accomplished without expense to the school authorities. Religion teachers of all creeds were merely offered the use of the public school classrooms for one period of between thirty and forty-five minutes once a week while the school was in session. Attendance records were required to be kept and reported to the school principal in the same manner as attendance at other school classes was required to be reported. The Court, with Justice Black again writing the majority opinion, agreed with Vashti McCollum that Champaign had created "an establishment of religion."

Fault was found not only with the fact that the public school buildings were used for the dissemination of religious doctrines but with the fact, really a conclusion drawn by the Court itself, that the state's compulsory education law (which mandated school attendance between the ages of seven and sixteen) afforded sectarian groups an "invaluable aid" in the teaching of their religion. The state provided a captive audience. Although no one compelled the child to receive religious instruction, he was in the public school because the state required him to be there—or at a state approved private school. And he could not escape unless he were an artful dodger, more sly of mind or fleet of foot than the truant officer.

Mr. Justice Reed, the lone dissenter in *McCollum*, found the Court's reference to Illinois' compulsory education law irrelevant. It is true that there was no immediate compulsion to receive religious instruction but the child was, if agnostic, subjected to embarrassment if he elected not to receive religious instruction at all or if, as a member of a minority creed, he elected not to follow the crowd. Of this apparent equation of embarrassment with compulsion Justice Reed wrote:

> Even assuming that certain children who did not elect to take instruction are embarrassed to remain outside of the classes, one can hardly speak of that embarrassment as a prohibition against the free exercise of religion. As no issue of prohibition upon the free exercise of religion is before us, we need only examine the School Board's action to see if it constitutes an establishment of religion. 333 U.S. at 241.

With that observation, Justice Black was eventually to agree. Fifteen years later, in Engel v. Vitale, 370 U.S. 421 (1962), he told us that coercion is not of the essence of Establishment. But, in *McCollum* itself he was careful to reaffirm his *Everson* dictum that the Establishment Clause forbids not only governmental preference of one religion over another but also an impartial governmental assistance for all religions. Even the dissenting justices in *Everson* subscribed to that construction. They disagreed only as to the application of the principle to the facts presented there.

Given that complete agreement on the principle, is it not evident that *McCollum* was an inevitable consequence of the *Everson* concurrences? The bus transportation, which Ewing Township financed for children attending church-related schools and which *Everson* sanctioned, served a secular purpose. The religious instruction presented in *McCollum* was exclusively religious. It served no secular purpose—unless we can say, in the Congressional common sense expressed in the Northwest Ordinance, that religion and morality are per se "necessary to good government and the happiness of mankind" or unless we accept the admonition of Jefferson that "the inculcation of the benevolence of God is essential to education if education is to produce moral men." R. Healey, Jefferson on Religion in Public Education, 160 (1962). Justice Black, however, ignored, and implicitly rejected, any such secular influence of religion. For that reason Zorach v. Clauson, supra, might read like an essay in semantics.

The New York released time program considered in *Zorach* was, quite obviously, purely religious in its motivation and design. Upon the written request of their parents, public school students were simply released, for no more than one hour a week, during the school day in order to attend out-of-school religious centers for religious instruction or devotional exercises. Those not released were required to remain in their classrooms. The churches or religious centers made weekly reports to the schools, sending a list of children who had been released from public school but who had not reported for religious instruction. The New York program had all the trappings of *McCollum*'s Champaign program with the solitary difference that New York's program was an out-of-school program while Champaign's was an in-school released time program. The Court found the New York system constitutional.

Writing for the majority, Mr. Justice Douglas said:

> This "released time" program involves neither religious instruction in public school classrooms nor the expenditure of public funds. All costs, including the application blanks, are paid by the religious organizations. The case is therefore unlike McCollum v. Board of Education * * *. In that case the classrooms were turned over to religious instructors. 343 U.S. at 308–309.

The Douglas distinction encompassed in the sentence, "All costs, including the application blanks, are paid by the religious organizations," is rather flawed, and it was left unexplained. *McCollum* had expressly stated that both the religious teachers and the permission cards were provided by the

Champaign Council on Religious Education, a private association, at no expense to the school authorities. 333 U.S. at 208. So, when Justice Douglas added, "We follow the McCollum case," 343 U.S. at 315, his logic became somewhat elusive.

Is the difference between *Zorach* and *McCollum* a difference without a distinction? Justice Douglas noted that in *McCollum* "the classrooms were turned over to religious instructors" and he returned to that thought in the concluding paragraph of his opinion. Was he measuring the degree of coercion brought to bear upon the captive public school youngster of pliable mind? It is true that the religious teachers in *McCollum* were offered the podium of the public school teacher, a position of secular authority from which they were empowered to command all the awesome respect which the public school teacher has at his or her command. That seems to be the critical factor which Mr. Justice Brennan, in a later case, found to differentiate *Zorach* from *McCollum*. After first putting aside any possible differences in public expenditures, he said:

> The deeper difference was that the McCollum program placed the religious instructor in the public school classroom in precisely the position of authority held by the regular teachers of secular subjects, while the Zorach program did not. The McCollum program, in lending to the support of sectarian instruction all the au-

thority of the governmentally operated public school system, brought government and religion into that proximity which the Establishment Clause forbids. To be sure, a religious teacher presumably commands substantial respect and merits attention in his own right. But the Constitution does not permit that prestige and capacity for influence to be augmented by investiture of all the symbols of authority at the command of the lay teacher for the enhancement of secular instruction. Abington School Dist. v. Schempp, 374 U.S. 203, 262–263 (1963) (Brennan, J., concurring).

Or was Justice Douglas tempering *Everson*'s and *McCollum*'s stern strictures on Establishment with a benevolent concern for the individual's right to the free exercise of his or her religion? Douglas spoke at first of the Free Exercise Clause but not expressly vis-a-vis the Establishment Clause. He said:

It takes obtuse reasoning to inject any issue of the "free exercise" of religion into the present case. * * *

There is a suggestion that the system involves the use of coercion to get public school students into religious classrooms. There is no evidence in the record before us that supports that conclusion. The present record indeed tells us that the school authorities are neutral in this regard and do no more than release students whose parents so request. If in fact coercion were used, if it were established that any one or more teachers were using their office to persuade or force students to take the religious instruction, a wholly different case would be presented. Hence we put aside that claim of coercion both as respects the "free exercise" of religion and "an establishment of religion" within the meaning of the First Amendment. 343 U.S. at 311-312.

Turning then to the Establishment Clause itself, he enumerated a dozen accepted areas of non-dependent—and non-entangling—cooperation between church and state. He wrote:

There cannot be the slightest doubt that the First Amendment reflects the philosophy that Church and State should be separated. * * * The First Amendment, however, does not say that in every and all respects there shall be a separation of Church and State. Rather, it studiously defines the manner, the specific ways, in which there shall be no concert or union or dependency one on the other. That is the common sense of the matter. Otherwise the state and religion would be aliens to each other—hostile, suspicious, and even unfriendly. Churches could not be required to pay even property taxes. Municipalities would not be permitted to render police or fire protection to religious groups. Policemen who helped parishioners into their places of worship would violate the Constitution. Prayers in our legislative halls; the appeals to the Almighty in the messages of the Chief Executive; the proclamations making Thanksgiving Day a holiday; "so help me God" in our courtroom oaths —these and all other references to the Almighty that run through our laws, our public rituals, our ceremonies would be flouting the First Amendment. A fastidious atheist or agnostic could even object to the supplication with which the Court opens each session: "God save the United States and this Honorable Court."

We would have to press the concept of separation of Church and State to these extremes to condemn the present law on constitutional grounds. The nullification of this law would have wide and profound effects. * * *

We are a religious people whose institutions presuppose a Supreme Being. We guarantee the freedom to worship as one chooses. We make room for as wide a variety of beliefs and creeds as the spiritual needs of man deem necessary. We sponsor an attitude on the part of government that shows no partiality to any one group and that lets each flourish according to the zeal of its adherents and the appeal of its dogma. When the state encourages religious instruction or cooperates with religious authorities by adjusting the schedule of public events to sectarian needs, it follows the best of our traditions. For it then respects the religious nature of our people and accommodates the public service to their spiritual needs. To hold that it may not would be to find in the Constitution a requirement that the government show a callous indifference to religious groups. That would be preferring those who believe in no religion over those who do believe. Government may not finance religious groups nor undertake religious instruction nor blend secular and sectarian education nor use secular institutions to force one or some religion on any person. But we find no constitutional requirement which makes it necessary for government to be hostile to religion and to throw its weight against efforts to widen the effective scope of religious influence. The government must be neutral when it comes to competition between sects. * * *

The problem, like many problems in constitutional law, is one of degree. 343 U.S. at 312–314.

Though Douglas repeated that the "constitutional standard is the separation of Church and State," a separation which "must be complete and unequivocal," 343 U.S. at 314, 312, those words, in retrospect, read like the exordium to an oration in which, with Ciceronian ease, he sought first to pacify the advocates of absolute separation only to beguile them into acceptance of a new and different principle. In his peroration he preached an "accommodations" doctrine, a neutrality between church and state, a concept which fostered a sociability quite at odds with the "high and impregnable wall" which *Everson* had designed and *McCollum* had constructed.

Despite *McCollum*'s absolutist application of the Establishment Clause, this was not an entirely novel homily Mr. Justice Douglas delivered. In *Everson*, Justice Black had stated, as a generalized principle, that the First Amendment "requires the state to be a neutral in its relations with groups of religious believers and non-believers." 330 U.S. at 18. This neutrality concept was eventually to surface in Abington School Dist. v. Schempp, supra, and in Walz v. Tax Comm'n, 397 U.S. 664 (1970), not as an Establishment-permitted accommodation between government and religion, but as a Free Exercise-mandated reconciliation of the religion clauses, "an accommodation of the Establishment and Free Exercise Clauses" to prevent "the kind of involvement that would tip the balance toward governmental control of churches or governmental restraint on religious practices." 397 U.S. at 669-670.

Schempp was even more specific. Its precept was a "wholesome 'neutrality' " between what "the

Establishment Clause prohibits" and what "the Free Exercise Clause guarantees." 374 U.S. at 222. Thus, as the Due Process Clause has been said to permit a little larceny now and then, such an "accommodation" might be found to tolerate a little Establishment now and then—to be justified as the inevitable consequence of protecting the Free Exercise of Religion.

Justice Black, though, did not consider it all that easy to reconcile *Zorach* with *McCollum*. Dissenting in *Zorach*, he found the Court's holdings contradictory. He also gave hint of a realistic explanation of *Zorach's* refined retreat from the *McCollum* rationale. Black noted that the "McCollum decision * * * has been subjected to a most searching examination throughout the country." 343 U.S. at 317. If by "searching examination" he meant searching and critical examination his reflection would have been both complete and correct. But, it would do a disservice to Mr. Justice Douglas to suggest that the *Zorach* Court was attuning the Constitution to the tempo of the times. It is true, however, that a most critical evaluation of the *McCollum* holding began in *McCollum* itself with the dissent of Mr. Justice Reed. Vigorously assailing the historical underpinnings of both the *Everson* and *McCollum* decisions, Justice Reed had written,

> [N]ever until today * * * has this Court widened its interpretation to any such degree

as holding that recognition of the interest of our nation in religion, through the granting, to qualified representatives of the principal faiths, of opportunity to present religion as an optional, extracurricular subject during released school time in public school buildings, was equivalent to an establishment of religion. A reading of the general statements of eminent statesmen of former days, referred to in the opinions in this case and in Everson v. Board of Education * * * will show that circumstances such as those in this case were far from the minds of the authors. The words and spirit of those statements may be wholeheartedly accepted without in the least impugning the judgment of the State of Illinois.

Mr. Jefferson, as one of the founders of the University of Virginia, a school which from its establishment in 1819 has been wholly governed, managed and controlled by the State of Virginia, was faced with the same problem that is before this Court today: the question of the constitutional limitation upon religious education in public schools. In his annual report as Rector, to the President and Directors of the Literary Fund, dated October 7, 1822, approved by the Visitors of the University of whom Mr. Madison was one, Mr. Jefferson set forth his views at some length. These suggestions of Mr. Jefferson were adopted and

[40]

* * * the Regulations of the University
* * * provided that: "Should the religious
sects of this State, or any of them, according
to the invitation held out to them, establish
within, or adjacent, to the precincts of the
University, schools for instruction in the religion of their sect, the students of the University will be free, and expected to attend religious worship at the establishment of their
respective sects, in the morning, and in time
to meet their school in the University at its
stated hours." Thus, the "wall of separation
between church and State" that Mr. Jefferson
built at the University which he founded did
not exclude religious education from that
school. The difference between the generality
of his statements on the separation of church
and state and the specificity of his conclusions
on education are considerable. A rule of law
should not be drawn from a figure of speech.

Mr. Madison's Memorial and Remonstrance
against Religious Assessments, relied upon by
the dissenting Justices in Everson, is not applicable here. Mr. Madison was one of the
principal opponents in the Virginia General
Assembly of a Bill Establishing a Provision
for Teachers of the Christian Religion. The
monies raised by the taxing section of that bill
were to be appropriated "by the Vestries, Elders,
or Directors of each religious society, * * *

[41]

to a provision for a Minister or Teacher of the Gospel of their denomination, or the providing places of divine worship, and to none other use whatsoever * * *." The conclusive legislative struggle over this act took place in the fall of 1785, before the adoption of the Bill of Rights. The Remonstrance had been issued before the General Assembly convened and was instrumental in the final defeat of the act, which died in committee. Throughout the Remonstrance, Mr. Madison speaks of the "establishment" sought to be effected by the act. It is clear from its historical setting and its language that the Remonstrance was a protest against an effort by Virginia to support Christian sects by taxation. Issues similar to those raised by the instant case were not discussed. Thus, Mr. Madison's approval of Mr. Jefferson's report as Rector gives, in my opinion, a clearer indication of his views on the constitutionality of religious education in public schools than his general statements on a different subject. 333 U.S. at 244–248.

(d) *McCollum's Critics*

Justice Reed's historical assessment of *McCollum* was expanded and turned into an analytical attack by Edward Corwin. § 2.01, supra. Professor Corwin candidly characterized Justice Black's homily on history as a distortion of history. In rather strong language he deplored the "eager crusaders on the Court [who] make too much of Jefferson's Danbury letter", 14 Law & Contemp.Prob. at 14, and who might aspire, in the words of Mr. Justice Jackson, to "the role of super board of education for every school district in the nation." Id. at 22.

The Journal of the American Bar Association was only slightly less restrained. In its June, 1948 issue it editorialized:

A month after the decision in the McCollum case, the Congress passed and the President signed an appropriation of $500,000 to erect a chapel for religions at the United States Merchant Marine Academy at King's Point, New York. On May 28 the United States Post Office placed on sale a postage stamp bearing the legend: "These Immortal Chaplains * * * Interfaith in Action." It bears portraits of four young ministers of religion—a Methodist, a Roman Catholic priest, a Jewish rabbi, and a Baptist—and also a painting of a torpedoed troop-ship which carried them to their graves off Greenland on February 3, 1943—the S.S. Dorchester of our Navy. They were on government property at taxpayers' expense, to hold religious services and give instruction and ministration in religion. And when they made their way to the deck of the stricken ship, they gave their life-jackets to four young men who had lost theirs in the confusion. Having given away their own chance to live, the four chaplains stood close together, holding hands, as the ship went under—an immortal demonstration of the unity of religious faiths and what religion does for people—now appropriately commemorated by our government. Was all this "constitutional"? Maybe there was something in the Dorchester incident which the majority in the Supreme Court [in the McCollum case] missed—something to which the highest Courts of our States and countless local communities have held fast.

The Constitution of the Soviet Union provides (Article 124): "In order to insure to citizens freedom of conscience, the church in the USSR is separated from the state, and the school from the church. Freedom of religious worship and freedom of anti-religious propaganda is recognized for all citizens."

Fortunately, the framers of our Constitution did not go that far, and the institutions and practices of our people have not gone that far. Nothing in our Constitution commands that the First Amendment should now be interpreted as though it read like the above-quoted provision. Nothing in our Constitution commands that "freedom of religion" shall be freedom *from* religion. 34 ABAJ 482, 484 (1948). (Emphasis in original).

These are but two illustrations of public reaction to the *McCollum* decision. This public reaction is briefly recited here to note that "realistic" evaluation of Zorach v. Clauson at which Justice Black hinted. It involved a sort of psychoanalysis of the *Zorach* majority. Though Mr. Justice Douglas wrote in *Zorach*, "We follow the McCollum case," some Court observers were quick to suggest that the Court had followed *McCollum* only to the judicial churchyard for a decent interment. The antique adage, "the Court reads the newspapers," was revarnished. It was said that the *Zorach* decision was a judicial reaction to public criticism of the Court and that the *Zorach* majority had, by a process of insufficient distinction, realistically overruled *McCollum* or had, at the very least, isolated it in its specific context. Reports of *McCollum*'s demise proved apocryphal. *McCollum* was alive and well ten years later when Engel v. Vitale, supra, was decided.

(e) Engel v. Vitale

Engel is the "Regents' Prayer case." The New York State Board of Regents, a body vested under the state constitution and by the state legislature with broad supervisory powers over the State's public school system had composed a prayer:

> Almighty God, we acknowledge our dependence upon Thee, and we beg Thy blessings upon us, our parents, our teachers and our Country.

The prayer, required to be said aloud by each class in the presence of a teacher at the beginning of each school day, was sustained, against an Establishment Clause challenge, by the New York state courts at the trial level, in the Appellate Division and in the Court of Appeals—"so long as the schools did not compel any pupil to join in the prayer over his or his parent's objection." The trial court had, in fact, mandated that regulations be adopted to make clear that "neither teacher nor any other school authority may comment on participation or nonparticipation in the exercise" and that nonparticipation "may take the form either of remaining silent during the exercise, or if the parent or child so desires, of being excused entirely from the exercise." Engel v. Vitale, 370 U.S. at 423–424, n. 2.

The Supreme Court reversed. For the Court, Mr. Justice Black wrote:

There can, of course, be no doubt that New York's program of daily classroom invocation of God's blessings as prescribed in the Regents' prayer is a religious activity. It is a solemn avowal of divine faith and supplication for the blessings of the Almighty. The nature of such a prayer has always been religious, none of the respondents has denied this and the trial court expressly so found * * *.

We agree with [petitioners'] contention since we think that the constitutional prohibition against laws respecting an establishment of religion must at least mean that in this country it is no part of the business of government to compose official prayers for any group of the American people to recite as a part of a religious program carried on by government.

* * *

Neither the fact that the prayer may be denominationally neutral nor the fact that its observance on the part of the students is voluntary can serve to free it from the limitations of the Establishment Clause, as it might from the Free Exercise Clause, of the First Amendment * * *. The Establishment Clause, unlike the Free Exercise Clause, does not depend upon any showing of direct governmental compulsion and is violated by the enactment of laws which establish an official religion whether those laws operate directly to coerce nonobserving individuals or not. This is not to say, of course, that laws officially prescribing a particular form of religious worship do not involve coercion of such individuals. When the power, prestige and financial support of government is placed behind a particular religious belief, the indirect coercive pressure upon religious minorities to conform to the prevailing officially approved religion is plain. But the purposes underlying the Establishment Clause go much further than that. Its first and most immediate purpose rested on the belief that a union of government and

[47]

religion tends to destroy government and to degrade religion. 370 U.S. at 424–431.

Black cited not a single Court decision in support of his conclusion. He chose to give us another lesson in history. Appropriately enough in this, a "prayer" case, he wrote first of the Book of Common Prayer, "created under governmental direction" and "approved by Acts of Parliament," which set out in "minute detail the accepted form and content of prayer and other religious ceremonies to be used in the established, tax-supported Church of England;" told us how "controversies over the Book and what should be its content repeatedly threatened to disrupt the peace" in England as "the accepted forms of prayer in the established church changed with the views of the particular ruler that happened to be in control at the time;" and noted that the "Puritans twice attempted to modify the Book of Common Prayer and once attempted to destroy it" until eventually they and other groups "decided to leave England and its established church and seek freedom in America from England's governmentally ordained and supported religion."

It is, of course, a fact of history that there was and is in England an established church and that the Church of England became the established church in at least five American colonies while in others the Congregationalist Church was officially established. There is no doubt that the men who wrote our Constitution and who framed the First Amendment rebelled against a Congressionally established church and perhaps with equal fervor against all state established churches. But it is difficult to equate the Regents' simple twenty-two word prayer with the Book of Common Prayer and more difficult to ˙equate its uncoerced recital with the establishment of an official state church. Mr. Justice Stewart was unpersuaded by the Court's perusal of history. In dissent he wrote:

I think the Court has misapplied a great constitutional principle. I cannot see how an "official religion" is established by letting those who want to say a prayer say it. On the contrary, I think that to deny the wish of these school children to join in reciting this prayer is to deny them the opportunity of sharing in the spiritual heritage of our Nation.

The Court's historical review of the quarrels over the Book of Common Prayer in England throws no light for me on the issue before us in this case. * * * Equally unenlightening, I think, is the history of the early establishment and later rejection of an official church in our own States. For we deal here not with the establishment of a state church, which would, of course, be constitutionally impermissible, but with whether school children who want to begin their day by joining in prayer must be prohibited from doing so. 370 U.S. at 445. (Stewart, J., dissenting).

Justice Black may also have recognized the inadequacy of his equation. He sought to give it substance, a substance expressed in a fear, not of what the Regents' Prayer had actually accomplished but of what official prayers might ultimately foster.

It is neither sacrilegious nor antireligious to say that each separate government in this country should stay out of the business of writing or sanctioning official prayers and leave that purely religious function to the people themselves and to those the people choose to look to for religious guidance.

It is true that New York's establishment of its Regents' prayer as an officially approved religious doctrine of that State does not amount to a total establishment of one particular religious sect to the exclusion of all others —that, indeed, the governmental endorsement of that prayer seems relatively insignificant when compared to the governmental encroachments upon religion which were commonplace 200 years ago. To those who may subscribe to the view that because the Regents' official prayer is so brief and general there can be no danger to religious freedom in its governmental establishment, however, it may be ap-

[50]

propriate to say in the words of James Madison, the author of the First Amendment:

"[I]t is proper to take alarm at the first experiment on our liberties * * *." 370 U.S. at 435–436.

(f) The Engel Eruption

Note has been taken of the tempest which followed in the wake of the *McCollum* decision. It is worth recalling, if only because Mr. Justice Black wrote in *Engel* that the "history of man is inseparable from the history of religion," that the *McCollum* tempest was but a gentle gust compared with the hurricane gale let loose by Engel v. Vitale. While President Kennedy, with executive decorum, urged public respect for the Court and observed that the proper place of prayer is in the home and church rather than in the public school, and while the only living former Presidents, Herbert C. Hoover, Harry S. Truman and Dwight D. Eisenhower, unemotionally stated that the Court had made a mistake, others—cleric and lay alike—agonized over the decision. The Cardinal Archbishop of New York called it "shocking" and the Methodist Bishop of California declared that the Court "has deconsecrated the nation." Congressman Becker of New York scored the ruling as "a grave disaster * * * the decision a sad day in the history of our country." Representative Ashmore, with obvious irony, introduced a bill which would have required that the words "In God

We Trust" be emblazoned in gold letters above the bench of the Supreme Court.

The reflex reactions of Representatives Becker and Ashmore are illustrative of Congressional repercussions which followed. Perhaps they reflected the sense of a startled society as well. For, while Congressmen may not be bookish beings, presumably they do read constituents' mail as well as the newspapers. It is enough to note, and safe to to say, that in both Houses of Congress there were explosive reactions. One need only skim the "manifesto" published in the name of ninety-six members of Congress, a vituperative attack on the Supreme Court, or count the number of bills introduced to restrict the Court's jurisdiction and to reverse the *Engel* decision, to sense the violence of the storm which erupted over the Supreme Court. Indeed, one sometimes wonders whether more time was not spent in protest than ever was spent in prayer, and more fervor found in conclaves called to damn the Court than ever was found in church or tabernacle.

That conjecture is not intended as an irreverent reciprocal criticism of the Court's critics nor is it intended to disparage their sincerity or to impugn their motives. Indeed, the ferment over *Engel* was not at all abnormal. For, *Zorach*'s calm now proved to be but a lull in the eye of the storm which had originated with *McCollum*. *Zorach*'s declaration, "We are a religious people whose institutions presuppose a Supreme Being. We guarantee the freedom to worship as one chooses," had received wide acclaim. The words had a breathless charm. Although per se they compelled no specific conclusion, they were idyllic—from a political point of view. And, beyond all that, recital of a prayer is certainly less embracive of religion than the religious indoctrination which McCollum had declared anathema—particularly when the outlawed prayer is the bland and insignificant little invocation which the Regents had seen fit to compose. Its sole religious virtue was that it "presupposed a Supreme Being" and even then it did so only for those who were willing to acknowledge the Almighty.

It was not unreasonable to argue, as a fair number of Court followers did, that *Engel*, by denying to those who chose to start the school day with a brief prayer, the opportunity to do so, had retracted the guarantee of "freedom to worship as one chooses." Dean Griswold of the Harvard Law School was of that number. He suggested that the Court had transformed our tradition of religious toleration into one of religious sterility.

Dean Griswold took aim at Justice Black's absolutist constitutional philosophy in general and the *Engel* decision in particular:

> I would like to suggest, with great respect, and real concern, that the Supreme Court of the United States has, in recent years, been

engaged, in certain types of cases, in a species of absolutism in its reasoning, which is more likely to lead us into darkness than to light.

* * *

Does our deep-seated tolerance of all religions—or, to the same extent, of no religion —require that we give up all religious observance in public activities? Why should it? It certainly never occurred to the Founders that it would. It is hardly likely that it was entirely accidental that these questions did not even come before the Court in the first hundred and fifty years of our constitutional history.

* * *

This is a country of religious toleration. That is a great consequence of our history embodied in the First Amendment. But does religious toleration mean religious sterility? Griswold, Absolute Is in the Dark—A Discussion of the Approach of the Supreme Court to Constitutional Questions, 8 Utah L.Rev. 167, 168–176 (1963).

He noted that this "has been, and is, a Christian country, in origin, history, tradition and culture", that it was out of Christian doctrine and ethics it "developed its notion of toleration;" asked, "does the fact that we have officially adopted toleration as our standard mean that we must give up our history and our tradition?" and challenged both the juridical and pedagogical merits of *Engel*.

> Let us consider the Jewish child, or the Catholic child, or the nonbeliever, or the Congregationalist, or the Quaker. He * * * attends a public school [which] has prescribed the Regents' prayer. When the prayer is recited, if this child or his parents feel that he cannot participate, he may stand or sit * * * while the other children take part in the ceremony. Or he may leave the room. It is said that this is bad, because it sets him apart from other children. * * * But is this the way it should be looked at? The child of a nonconforming or minority group is, to be sure, different in his beliefs. That is what it means to be a member of a minority. Is it not desirable, and educational, for him to learn and observe this, in the atmosphere of the school—not so much that he is different, as that other children are different from him? And is it not desirable that, at the same time, he experiences and learns the fact that his difference is tolerated and accepted? No compulsion is put upon him. He need not participate. But he, too, has the opportunity to be tolerant. He allows the majority of the group to follow their own tradition, perhaps coming to understand and to respect what they feel is significant to them. Id. at 177.

(g) The Significance of Engel

Several observations may be made of Dean Griswold's evaluation of *Engel*. First, if there were cause for "concern" the cause really arose in 1947. For, accepting the philosophy of *Everson* and its application in *McCollum*, *Engel* was inevitable. In *McCollum* the Court found "an establishment" in the religious instruction given in a public elementary school to those who chose to be so instructed. The Court there condemned state laws or local rules designed to promote religion in preference to irreligion. If, as *McCollum* found, the *teaching* of religion serves no secular purpose how could the recitation of a prayer, howsoever nondenominational, be anything if not exclusively religious in purpose, in essence and in effect?

Secondly, it bears renoting that in his *Engel* opinion Mr. Justice Black made no reference either to *Everson* or to *McCollum* or to any other decision of the Court. What was condemned by the Court was the *writing* by the Board of Regents of an *official* prayer. It is "no part of the business of government to compose official prayers," he said. And he repeated that precept, "each separate government in this country should stay out of the business of writing or sanctioning official prayers." This is the essence of the *Engel* holding. So, no shadow of unconstitutionality was cast upon Thanksgiving proclamations, a traditional Presidential practice, or upon other official exhortations to

[56]

pray as one may choose to pray. He also observed, however, that the Regents' Prayer was "a solemn avowal of divine faith and supplication for the blessings of the Almighty" and that the "nature of such a prayer has always been religious." Prayer, in brief, is a religious exercise and it is exclusively religious. At the same time Justice Black was careful to note:

> There is of course nothing in the decision reached here that is inconsistent with the fact that school children and others are officially encouraged to express love for our country by reciting historical documents such as the Declaration of Independence which contain references to the Deity or by singing officially espoused anthems which include the composer's professions of faith in a Supreme Being, or with the fact that there are many manifestations in our public life of belief in God. Such patriotic or ceremonial occasions bear no true resemblance to the unquestioned religious exercise that the State of New York has sponsored in this instance. 370 U.S. at 435, n. 21.

Thus, the secular-religious dichotomy was at least implicit in *Engel*. Though the fact remained that state officials composed *Engel's* invocation, no state official, whatever his religious experience or canonical expertise, could lay claim to authorship of the Lord's Prayer or of any of the books of the

Bible. It remained for Abington School Dist. v. Schempp (Pennsylvania), supra, and Murray v. Curlett (Maryland), its conjoined case, to face the issue of non-official prayers in public schools.

(h) *Abington School Dist. v. Schempp—A Two-Tier Test*

By statute, the Commonwealth of Pennsylvania had mandated the reading aloud, without comment, of at least ten verses from the Holy Bible at the opening of public school on each school day. In *Abington School District* the reading was followed by a standing recital of the Lord's Prayer. Students and their parents were advised that any student was free to absent himself from the classroom or, should he elect to remain, not to participate in the exercises. In Baltimore, Maryland, the Board of School Commissioners adopted a rule providing for the holding of opening exercises in the public schools of the city, consisting primarily of the "reading, without comment, of a chapter in the Holy Bible and/or the use of the Lord's Prayer." There, too, children could be excused from the exercise on request of the parent. The Court was unperturbed by *Engel*'s protestors. It followed the *Everson—McCollum—Engel* trail. With but one dissent, both practices in each state and each school district were declared unconstitutional.

Mr. Justice Clark, who wrote the majority opinion, did not weary us with additional history readings. He accepted history as the Court had pre-

sented it in its prior decisions. Unlike Mr. Justice
Black in *Engel*, he cited cases, both Free Exercise
and Establishment decisions, and with lawyer-like
adherence to the doctrine of stare decisis he concluded:

> These exercises are prescribed as part of the
> curricular activities of students who are re-
> quired by law to attend school. They are held
> in the school buildings under the supervision
> and with the participation of teachers employ-
> ed in those schools. None of these factors,
> other than compulsory school attendance, was
> present in the program upheld in Zorach v.
> Clauson. The trial court * * * has found
> that such an opening exercise is a religious
> ceremony and was intended by the State to be
> so. We agree with the trial court's finding as
> to the religious character of the exercises.
> Given that finding, the exercises and the law
> requiring them are in violation of the Estab-
> lishment Clause. 374 U.S. at 223.

In brief, there was no secular purpose in, or
secular reason for, the "religious" recitations in
Schempp. Justice Clark expanded on that simple
finding. He harmonized—again with devotion to
stare decisis—the historical soundings which had
been echoing in the Court's decisions since Reynolds v. United States, 98 U.S. 145 (1879), Bradfield v.
Roberts, supra, and Everson v. Board of Educ.

The singular test of Establishment, that of serving a secular purpose he restated as a two-pronged test.

> The test may be stated as follows: what are the purpose and the primary effect of the enactment? If either is the advancement or inhibition of religion then the enactment exceeds the scope of legislative power as circumscribed by the Constitution. That is to say that to withstand the strictures of the Establishment Clause there must be a secular legislative purpose and a primary effect that neither advances nor inhibits religion. 374 at 222.

Thus, the Court refused to confine *Engel*'s holding to the composition of state prayers by state officials. Had it been so confined, biblical readings, including the Lord's Prayer, would have presented an essentially different case. But *Engel*'s message was read to proscribe all public school exercises which are exclusively religious. As such they provide a preference for religion over nonreligion. In brief, all prayers in public schools are impermissible and public schools are Constitutionally compelled to be exclusively secular. This was the ultimate religious sterilization of the public school which the precocious Dean Griswold had already deprecated. It is the inexorable consequence of the *McCollum—Engel—Schempp* triology.

Justice Clark's duplex formula was relatively easy to apply in *Schempp*. Once found, as the trial court had, that the opening exercise was "a religious ceremony and was intended by the State to be so," there was no secular legislative purpose in either the reading of the biblical verses or the recital of the Lord's Prayer. There would be, or certainly could be, a secular legislative purpose in the study of the *history* of Judas Maccabaeus, the Canticle of Canticles as a *poetic* exercise, or the Lord's Prayer for its concise *literary* construction. And in that context each would have, or could have, a primary secular effect. Mr. Justice Clark seemed to think so. In a dictum, he wrote:

> [I]t might well be said that one's education is not complete without a study of comparative religion or the history of religion and its relationship to the advancement of civilization. It certainly may be said that the Bible is worthy of study for its literary and historic qualities. Nothing we have said here indicates that such study of the Bible or of religion, when presented objectively as part of a secular program of education, may not be effected consistently with the First Amendment. But the exercises here do not fall into those categories. They are religious exercises, required by the States in violation of the command of the First Amendment that the Government main-

tain strict neutrality, neither aiding nor opposing religion.   374 U.S. at 225.

(i) The Test Applied—Board of Education v. Allen

The Clark restatement of the Establishment standard in terms of purpose and effect was reaffirmed in Board of Educ. v. Allen, 392 U.S. 236 (1968). *Allen* returned, for the first time since *Everson*, to the issue of aid to parochial schools. Now the Court focused on New York's lending of state approved secular textbooks free of charge to all students in grades seven to twelve, including those in private schools. The Constitutionality of the New York law was challenged insofar as it authorized the loan of textbooks to students attending parochial schools. This was the Establishment issue which the Court had ignored in Cochran v. Louisiana, supra, and which *Everson* had inferentially, but only obliquely, approved.

Applying the *Schempp* rule, Mr. Justice White concluded, over the dissents of Justices Black and Douglas, that the New York law, like the New Jersey law in *Everson*, had "a secular legislative purpose and a primary effect that neither advances nor inhibits religion." He reasoned,

> The express purpose   *   *   *   was stated by the New York Legislature to be furtherance of the educational opportunities available to the young. Appellants have shown us nothing about the necessary effects of the statute that

[62]

is contrary to its stated purpose. * * *
[N]o funds or books are furnished to parochial
schools, and the financial benefit is to parents
and children, not to schools. Perhaps free
books make it more likely that some children
choose to attend a sectarian school, but that
was true of the state-paid bus fares in Everson and does not alone demonstrate an unconstitutional degree of support for a religious
institution.

Of course books are different from buses.
Most bus rides have no inherent religious significance, while religious books are common.
However, [the statute] does not authorize the
loan of religious books, and the State claims
no right to distribute religious literature. Although the books loaned are those required by
the parochial school for use in specific courses,
each book loaned must be approved by the
public school authorities; only secular books
may receive approval. * * * Absent evidence, we cannot assume that school authorities, who constantly face the same problem in
selecting textbooks for use in the public
schools, are unable to distinguish between secular and religious books or that they will not
honestly discharge their duties under the law.
* * *

The major reason offered by appellants for
distinguishing free textbooks from free bus

fares is that books, but not buses, are critical to the teaching process, and in a sectarian school that process is employed to teach religion. However this Court has long recognized that religious schools pursue two goals, religious instruction and secular education.

* * *

Against this background of judgment and experience, unchallenged in the meager record before us in this case, we cannot agree with appellants either that all teaching in a sectarian school is religious or that the processes of secular and religious training are so intertwined that secular textbooks furnished to students by the public are in fact instrumental in the teaching of religion. 392 U.S. at 243–248.

To "the parochial school problem" the Court did not return until Lemon v. Kurtzman, 403 U.S. 602, in 1971, the year which marked the beginning of the Constitutional decline and fall of governmental aid to church-related primary and secondary schools. In the interim the question of real estate tax exemptions for churches was benignly resolved in the churches' favor, Walz v. Tax Comm'n, supra. Mr. Chief Justice Burger's opinion was to have a substantial influence in subsequent decisions of the Court.

(j) Walz v. Tax Commission—the Non-Entanglement Principle

The Chief Justice noted at the outset in *Walz* that "for the men who wrote the Religion Clauses of the First Amendment the 'establishment' of a religion connoted sponsorship, financial support and active involvement of the sovereign in religious activity." He noted the inherent tension between the Establishment and Free Exercise Clauses, the "considerable internal inconsistency in the opinions of the Court" and the struggle "to find a neutral course between the two Religion Clauses, both of which are cast in absolute terms, and either of which, if expanded to a logical extreme would tend to clash with each other." He reaffirmed the principle of *Everson,* the accommodations of *Zorach* and the holding of *Allen.* And, albeit without citation of *Schempp,* he wrote in terms of the latter's duplex purpose and effect standard of Establishment.

He wrote, however, not of Establishment per se but of the "Religion Clauses of the First Amendment." One sensed that he recognized a need to retool the *Schempp* test, if due respect were to be given to the tax exemption laws in effect in "all of the 50 states" and to a practice which has been a part of "our national life, beginning with pre-Revolutionary colonial times."

> The general principle deducible from the First Amendment and all that has been said by the

Court is this: that we will not tolerate either governmentally established religion or governmental interference with religion. Short of those expressly proscribed governmental acts there is room for play in the joints productive of a benevolent neutrality which will permit religious exercise to exist without sponsorship and without interference.

Each value judgment under the Religion Clauses must therefore turn on whether particular acts in question are intended to establish or interfere with religious beliefs and practices or have the effect of doing so. Adherence to the policy of neutrality that derives from an accommodation of the Establishment and Free Exercise Clauses has prevented the kind of involvement that would tip the balance toward government control of churches or governmental restraint on religious practice.
* * *

No perfect or absolute separation is really possible; the very existence of the Religion Clauses is an involvement of sorts—one that seeks to mark boundaries to avoid excessive entanglement. 397 U.S. at 669-670.

Just as *Allen* had found a secular legislative purpose and a primary secular effect in the secular education which parochial schools provide, *Walz* might have focused on the eleemosynary or public welfare endeavors of the churches—such as child care, family counselling, aid to the poor, the elderly and the ill. Surely, in their public welfare pursuits the churches serve secular ends. *Allen*'s textbooks, however, were secular texts whose *primary* effect was the support of secular subjects and whose direct "financial benefit" was "to parents and children, not to schools." Aid which might have reached the religious function of the parochial schools was incidental or secondary, existing, if at all, only because free books might "make it more likely that some children choose to attend a sectarian school." A tax exemption, though negative by nature, is a form of financial support. If it were to be admeasured to the public welfare pursuits of the churches, would each church each year be required to submit a balance sheet reconciling the income value of the tax exemption with the cost of its secular services? Chief Justice Burger acknowledged that latent possibility but declined the invitation to engage in the practice of accounting.

> We find it unnecessary to justify the tax exemption on the social welfare services or "good works" that some churches perform for parishioners and others—family counselling, aid to the elderly and the infirm, and to children. Churches vary substantially in the scope of such services; programs expand or contract according to resources and need. As public-sponsored programs enlarge, private aid

from the church sector may diminish. The extent of social services may vary, depending on whether the church serves an urban or rural, a rich or poor constituency. To give emphasis to so variable an aspect of the work of religious bodies would introduce an element of governmental evaluation and standards as to the worth of particular social welfare programs, thus producing a kind of continuing day-to-day relationship which the policy of neutrality seeks to minimize. Hence, the use of a social welfare yardstick as a significant element to qualify for tax exemption could conceivably give rise to confrontations that could escalate to constitutional dimensions. 397 U.S. at 674.

Once the social welfare yardstick had been discarded, the issue so candidly presented was the validity of tax exemptions of churches used solely for religious exercises, of religion qua religion. Thus, the apparent need for retooling, or clarifying, *Schempp*'s test of Establishment. The first prong of the *Schempp* rubric was stated in terms of a "secular" legislative purpose. While the other prong postulated a primary effect which "neither advances nor inhibits religion," the accent was on the secular and, taken in its entirety, the *Schempp* rule seemed to require some resulting secular achievement. That is the sense in which it was applied in *Allen.* Now, in *Walz,* Chief Justice

[68]

Burger softened the secular tone of *Schempp* and *Allen*. His emphasis was not on whether the legislative purpose was to promote "secular" ends but whether the purpose was one which "neither advances nor inhibits religion"—a restatement certainly more flexible and less formidable if tax exemptions for the purely religious were to be sustained.

Walz's deemphasis of the secular, it is fair to say, was deliberate, and it was something more than a semantic by-play. But, it is not a contradiction to suggest in the same breath that *Walz* did not abandon *Schempp*'s two-pronged test. Indeed, it was repeated verbatim by Chief Justice Burger, less than one year later, in Lemon v. Kurtzman, supra. Acceptance of *Walz* as an affirmation of *Schempp*, or more accurately as an affirmation of the latter's phrasing of the Establishment test, underscores the double significance of the *Walz* holding and of the Court's rationale. It not only gave us a professedly principled illustration of what constitutes a secular legislative purpose and a novel illustration of what constitutes a primary or principal effect which neither advances nor inhibits religion; it also planted a non-entanglement seed which was to blossom in *Lemon* as the third bough of a tripartite test of Establishment.

Respecting the state's legislative purpose, *Walz* reasoned that New York had not singled out churches as such but, rather, had granted exemption to "all houses of religious worship within a broad class of property owned by nonprofit, quasi-public corporations which include hospitals, libraries, playgrounds, scientific, professional, historical, and patriotic groups." It noted that the State "has an affirmative policy that considers these groups as beneficial and stabilizing influences in community life and finds this classification useful, desirable and in the public interest" and that New York had determined that these entities, which exist "in a harmonious relationship to the community at large" and foster its "moral and mental improvement," should not "be inhibited in their activities by property taxation or the hazard of loss of those properties for nonpayment of taxes." The legislative intent, therefore, was not to aid religion qua religion but rather to benefit charitable or "public interest" societies in general—a purpose which cannot be characterized as non-secular simply because religious organizations are within the favored category of institutions.

The "secular" effect was found in the avoidance of excessive entanglement of government with religion. Elimination of exemption would "tend to expand the involvement of government" with religion "by giving rise to tax valuations of church property, tax liens, tax foreclosures and direct confrontations and conflicts that follow in the train of those legal processes." In its end result a property

tax exemption restricts "the fiscal relationship between church and state, and tends to complement
and reinforce the desired separation insulating
each from the other."

This avoidance of excessive entanglement was, as
noted, turned by *Lemon* into a third and separate
test of Establishment,

> Three such tests may be gleaned from our
> cases. First, the statute must have a secular
> legislative purpose; second, its principal or
> primary effect must be one that neither ad-
> vances nor inhibits religion * * *; finally,
> the statute must not foster "an excessive gov-
> ernment entanglement with religion." 403
> U.S. at 612–613.

(k) Lemon v. Kurtzman—The Tripartite Test

Lemon v. Kurtzman, on appeal from the United
States District Court for the Eastern District of
Pennsylvania, was decided (one year after Walz)
together with Earley v. DiCenso and Robinson v.
DiCenso, both on appeal from the United States
District Court for the District of Rhode Island.
The two appeals raised questions as to Pennsylvania and Rhode Island statutes providing state aid to
church-related elementary and secondary schools.
The Pennsylvania program furnished financial support to nonpublic elementary and secondary
schools by way of reimbursement for the cost of
teachers' salaries, textbooks, and instructional ma-

terials in specified secular subjects. Under the Rhode Island plan the State paid directly to teachers of secular subjects in nonpublic elementary schools a supplement of 15% of their annual salaries.

The statutes were different insofar as the Rhode Island payment went directly to nonpublic school teachers while Pennsylvania "purchased" a package of specified "secular educational services" from the nonpublic school and the purchase price was paid to the schools themselves. Both statutes were alike in that they rested on a legislative finding that the quality of education available in nonpublic schools (elementary in Rhode Island, elementary and secondary in Pennsylvania) had been jeopardized by rapidly rising salaries needed to attract competent and dedicated teachers. And each expressed a legislative desire to enhance the quality of secular education in all schools covered by the state's compulsory education laws. It was an obviously laudable purpose and one which a state legislature could, with Constitutional propriety, seek to accomplish. But, in the candid and careful structuring of their statutes to insure that only the secular segment of sectarian school education received the state's financial support, both legislatures tripped over what now became the third part of the tripartite test of Establishment—excessive government entanglement with religion. With only one dissent, both statutes were declared un-constitutional.

Chief Justice Burger wrote the Court's opinion and again, as in *Walz*, he wrote for a majority of the Court. He analyzed each statute separately but first laid down principles applicable to both. He found no reason to suppose that either legislature meant anything else than what it expressly stated as its reason for enacting its statute —enhancement of the quality of secular education. A state always "has a legitimate concern for main-itaining minimum standards in all schools it allows to operate" and, as there is "nothing here that undermines the stated legislative intent" it must, therefore, "be accorded appropriate deference." Deferentially, then, and succintly, each statute's secular purpose was accepted.

Did either, or both, statutes produce a principal or primary effect which neither advances nor inhibits religion? The Court chose not to answer that question. It professed to by-pass the second part of the then bifurcated test of Establishment as a needless exercise because both programs, substantially on evidence before the lower court in the Rhode Island case, failed what the Court now formulated as part three of a tripartite test. Both programs were found to foster an excessive government entanglement with religion. Because of its profound impact on subsequent parochial school cases the Court's analysis merits something more than a summary statement.

The Chief Justice first looked back to *Allen* and to the premises underlying the Rhode Island and Pennsylvania programs.

> In *Allen* the Court acknowledged that secular and religious teachings were not necessarily so intertwined that secular textbooks furnished to students by the State were in fact instrumental in the teaching of religion. * * * The legislatures of Rhode Island and Pennsylvania have concluded that secular and religious education are identifiable and separable. In the abstract we have no quarrel with this conclusion.

> The two legislatures, however, have also recognized that church-related elementary and secondary schools have a significant religious mission and that a substantial portion of their activities is religiously oriented. They have therefore sought to create statutory restrictions designed to guarantee the separation between secular and religious educational functions and to ensure that State financial aid supports only the former. All these provisions are precautions taken in candid recognition that these programs approached, even if they did not intrude upon, the forbidden areas under the Religion Clauses. We need not decide whether these legislative precautions restrict

the principal or primary effect of the programs to the point where they do not offend the Religion Clauses, for we conclude that the cumulative impact of the entire relationship arising under the statutes in each State involves excessive entanglement between government and religion.   403 U.S. at 613–614.

Of course, under the statutory exemption before the Court in *Walz*, "the State had a continuing burden to ascertain that the exempt property was in fact being used for religious worship."   But, "[j]udicial caveats against entanglement must recognize that the line of separation, far from being a 'wall', is a blurred, indistinct, and variable barrier depending on all the circumstances of a particular relationship."   So, from the candid acknowledgment of the "dual mission" of church-related elementary and secondary school the Court outlined, at least for those schools, its test of excessive entanglement:

In order to determine whether the government entanglement with religion is excessive, we must examine the character and purpose of the institutions that are benefited, the nature of the aid that the State provides, and the resulting relationship between the government and the religious authority.   403 U.S. at 615.

What, then, were the character and the purpose of the Pennsylvania and the Rhode Island church-related schools? What was the nature of the aid which those states provided? And what was the resulting relationship between the government and the religious authority? The nature of the aid was purely financial, a salary supplement paid directly to teachers in Rhode Island's nonpublic elementary schools and payment for secular services made directly to Pennsylvania's nonpublic elementary and secondary schools. That much was evident. But, from its assessment of the purpose and character of those schools the Court, painting with quick, bold strokes, produced a portrait or profile of a parochial school radiant with inevitable entanglement. The *Lemon* profile was crucial to, if not conclusive of, the Court's decision, and its impact on governmental programs of aid for every church-related school—and, indeed, for all nonpublic primary and secondary schools—was enormous.

(l) Lemon's Profile of the Parochial School—The Inevitable Entanglement

In the Rhode Island case (Earley v. DiCenso) the District Court had made extensive findings respecting the religious character of, and the purpose served by Rhode Island's Roman Catholic elementary schools—which to the date of the District Court's decision were the only schools whose lay teachers sought benefits under the Salary Supplement Act. The findings were indeed extensive. The church schools involved were located close to churches, thus providing convenient access for religious exercises to supplement "instruction in faith and morals" which is "part of the total educational process." The school buildings contained identifying religious symbols on the exterior and religious paintings and statutes in classrooms and hallways. Although only approximately thirty minutes a day were devoted to direct religious instructions, there were religiously oriented extracurricular activities. Approximately two-thirds of the teachers were nuns whose "dedicated efforts provide an atmosphere in which religious instruction and religious vocations are natural and proper parts of life in such schools" and, in acknowledgment of the role of teaching nuns in enhancing the religious atmosphere, the diocese had promulgated a policy of maintaining a minimum one-to-one ratio between nuns and lay teachers in all schools. 403 U.S. at 615–616.

On the basis of these findings the District Court concluded that the parochial schools constituted "an integral part of the religious mission of the Catholic Church" and that the various characteristics of the school made them "a powerful vehicle for transmitting the Catholic faith to the next generation." This process of inculcating religious doctrine, Chief Justice Burger added, was enhanced by the impressionable age of pupils, particularly in primary schools. 403 U.S. at 616.

The record further showed that Rhode Island's Roman Catholic elementary schools were under the general supervision of the Bishop of Providence. With only two exceptions school principals were nuns. A diocesan edict required that prospective lay teachers be interviewed first by the Diocesan Superintendent of Schools, and then by the school principal, and that all contracts of employment be signed by the parish priest who retained discretion in negotiating salary levels. The Court concluded that "[r]eligious authority necessarily pervades the school system." 403 U.S. at 617.

Course content was also a critical concern. The schools were governed "by the standards set forth in a 'Handbook of School Regulations,' which has the force of synodal law in the diocese." The Handbook in evidence emphasized the role of the teacher, stated that "[r]eligious formation is not confined to formal courses, nor is it restricted to a single subject area", and advised teachers to stimulate interest in religious vocations and missionary work. 403 U.S. at 618.

In accepting the District Court's factual conclusion that religious formulation was not restricted to a single subject area, the Chief Justice wrote, of course, of a specific Catholic elementary school system in the state of Rhode Island. Mr. Justice Douglas, in a separate opinion, was apparently unprepared to confine his comments to Rhode Island or to Pennsylvania. Quoting from Catholic as well as non-Catholic authorities, he generalized that in Catholic parochial schools Roman Catholic indoctrination is included in every subject and that "religion permeates the whole curriculum, and is not confined in a single half-hour period of the day." 403 U.S. at 635 (Douglas, J., concurring).

The Court's profile of the Rhode Island parochial school was reproduced as representative of church-related elementary and secondary schools in Pennsylvania—even though in the Pennsylvania case there was no hearing below, no factual findings, no testimony taken, no documentation offered. The Pennsylvania case reached the Supreme Court on direct appeal from the judgment of a three-judge district court dismissing the complaint for failure to state a claim for relief. The Supreme Court accepted as true the allegations of the complaint, as it must for purposes of a motion to dismiss. The complaint had in fact alleged that the Pennsylvania act "finances and participates in the blending of sectarian and secular education." Lemon v. Kurtzman, 310 F.Supp. 35, 43, n.15 (E.D.Pa.1969). Chief Justice Burger apparently considered that ambiguous allegation to be an advancement of a legal theory not required to be taken as true for purposes of a motion to dismiss. He read the complaint as asserting only three factual allegations, "the church-related elementary and secondary schools are controlled by religious organizations, have the purpose of propagating a particular religious faith, and conduct their operations to fulfill that purpose." From these allegations—thus bereft of any specific assertion that sectarian teaching invaded or would invade either course content or secular classes supported by state funds—the Supreme Court concluded, "The complaint describes an educational system that is very similar to the one existing in Rhode Island." 403 U.S. at 620.

There is, of course, an identifiable difference between the Court's profile of a parochial school and the Douglas concept of a permeated Catholic school. The former accentuates the religious environment, the external and internal atmosphere created in the parochial school by those of a particular religious faith. The latter finds an actual blending of sectarian and secular subjects, of sectarian and secular teaching in the parochial school. There is also a difference between the descriptive and detailed portrait of the Rhode Island Catholic parochial school system—a picture which Justice Douglas, painting with bolder strokes, turned into something akin to a caricature, 403 U.S. at 637–640 —and the *Lemon* complaint's impressionistic portrayal of Pennsylvania's church-related schools.

The church-related school systems in Rhode Island and in Pennsylvania were alike, however, insofar as each was controlled and operated by religious organizations for the purpose of propagating a particular religious faith. Given these condensed characteristics there was no need to find *actual* religious permeation of secular subjects or secular teaching. There was present, the Court concluded, a *potential* for permeation and that potential was the initial, but crucial Constitutional infirmity in each case. With the gloss of the "potential" added, it was not difficult to discern in the background of each portrait a vision of the aid-seeking parochial school twisting slowly, slowly in the wind.

Perhaps because his conclusion contradicted the evidentiary findings of the District Court in *Di Censo*, and thus proceeded from an undocumented premise, Chief Justice Burger took particular care in expounding this newly discovered mandate of the Establishment Clause. He wrote:

> Several teachers testified, however, that they did not inject religion into their secular classes. And the District Court found that religious values did not necessarily affect the content of the secular instruction. * * *

> We need not and do not assume that teachers in parochial schools will be guilty of bad faith or any conscious design to evade the limitations imposed by the statute and the First Amendment. We simply recognize that a dedicated religious person, teaching in a school affiliated with his or her faith and operated to inculcate its tenets, will inevitably experience great difficulty in remaining religiously neutral. Doctrines and faith are not inculcated or advanced by neutrals. With the best of inten-

tions such a teacher would find it hard to make a total separation between secular teaching and religious doctrine. * * *

We do not assume, however, that parochial school teachers will be unsuccessful in their attempts to segregate their religious beliefs from their secular educational responsibilities. But the potential for impermissible fostering of religion is present. The Rhode Island Legislature has not, and could not provide state aid on the basis of a mere assumption that secular teachers under religious discipline can avoid conflicts. The State must be certain, given the Religion Clauses, that subsidized teachers do not inculcate religion * * *. 403 U.S. at 618–619.

Rhode Island had manifestly undertaken to insure that "subsidized teachers [did] not inculcate religion." To that end it had conditioned its aid with "pervasive restrictions." An eligible recipient was permitted to teach only those courses which were offered in public schools, and to use only those texts and materials used in public schools and he was not permitted to engage in teaching any course in religion. Pennsylvania imposed similar restrictions. In addition to limiting reimbursement to courses offered in the public schools and materials approved by state officials, the Pennsylvania statute excluded "any subject matter expressing religious teaching, or the morals or forms of worship of any sect." Precisely because each state had sought so carefully to confine its charity to the secular service of the church-related schools, each became fatally entangled with religion. The Court held:

> A comprehensive, discriminating, and continuing state surveillance will inevitably be required to ensure that these restrictions are obeyed and the First Amendment otherwise respected. Unlike a book, a teacher cannot be inspected once so as to determine the extent and intent of his or her personal beliefs and subjective acceptance of the limitations imposed by the First Amendment. These prophylactic contacts will involve excessive and enduring entanglement between state and church. 403 U.S. at 619.

There was "another area of entanglement" which caused the Court "concern." The Rhode Island statute excluded teachers employed by nonpublic schools wherein the average per-pupil expenditures on secular education equalled or exceeded the comparable figures for public schools. In the event expenditures of an otherwise eligible school exceeded the norm, the State Commissioner of Education was required to examine the school's records to determine how much of the total expenditures was attributable to secular education and how much to religious activity. Similarly, under the Pennsylvania program schools seeking reimbursement were required to maintain such accounting procedures as would facilitate performance of the State's duty to establish the cost of the secular as distinguished from the religious instruction. "This kind of state inspection and evaluation of the religious content of a religious organization" the Court found to be "fraught with the sort of entanglement that the Constitution forbids" and "pregnant with dangers of excessive government direction of church schools and hence of churches." And, the government's post-audit powers "to inspect and evaluate a church-related school's financial records and to determine which expenditures are religious and which are secular creates an intimate and continuing relationship between church and state." 403 U.S. at 620–621.

Primarily and essentially, however, it was the spectre of state agents, like so many Inspectors Poirot, policing the content of courses in pursuit of incriminating evidence of religious indoctrination, which doomed both programs. Each state's involvement with religion was magnified by the necessary presence of state accountants commissioned to put a value upon, and to segregate the costs of, the secular and religious aspects of the educational program offered in the church-related schools. The Pennsylvania statute was flawed in another respect. It offered financial aid directly to the church-related schools. Distinguishing *Everson* and *Allen*, wherein "the Court was careful to point out that state aid was provided to the student and his parents—not to the church-related school," Chief Justice Burger reiterated the *Walz* warning,

> Obviously a direct money subsidy would be a relationship pregnant with involvement and, as with most governmental grant programs, could encompass sustained and detailed administrative relationships for enforcement of statutory or administrative standards   *   *   *.
> 403 U.S. at 621.

Finally, the Court found additional indicia of entanglement, "[a] broader base of entanglement of yet a different character   *   *   *   presented by the divisive political potential of these state programs." The Chief Justice envisaged a second spectre—of creeds in competition, importuning state legislatures for ever-increasing aid for their church-related schools, of political partisanship drawn along religious lines. Such "political division along religious lines," the Court declared, "was one of the principal evils against which the First Amendment was intended to protect." 403 U.S. at 622. This frightful vision of Christmas Yet To Come, its historical validity and its consequences, will be given a little more attention in a succeeding section. See § 2.05, infra.

(m) The Impact of Lemon

Lemon's impact fell upon the nonpublic elementary and secondary schools and only upon those schools. The Court did not disturb, for example, the church tax exemptions which *Walz* had approved. Indeed only an inconstant Court would dare do so only one year after its *Walz* decision. So, though *Lemon* equated the parochial school with the church itself—a living, organic part of the church mission to spread the faith of the church, to proselytize, to inculcate religion even in the teaching of secular subjects—and though the tax exemptions sanctioned in *Walz* secured for religion itself a sizeable measure of financial support, Chief Justice Burger fashioned an acceptable reconciliation of the two cases.

State tax exemptions for real property owned by religious organizations and used for religious worship, he wrote in *Lemon*, "tended to confine rather than enlarge the area of permissible state involvement with religious institutions" while salary supplements for parochial school teachers created an area wherein a "comprehensive, discriminating and continuing state surveillance" of their teaching would inevitably be required. And, he added that our long history of state tax exemptions for *all* places of religious worship, a practice "imbedded in our colonial experience and continuing into the present," stands in contrast to governmental funding of church-related schools, a relatively new phenomenon, which benefits only a relatively few religious groups. In the abstract that distinction might seem at odds with the *Everson* dictate that government cannot pass laws "which aid one religion, aid all religions, or prefer one religion over another," but it does accentuate the Court's foreboding fear that appeals for successive annual appropriations, growing larger and larger as inflation escalates and populations grow, for the "relatively few religious groups" would create political entanglement of church and state and intensify divisiveness on religious lines. History has taught us that tax exemptions are not divisive, either along political or along religious lines, and there is no present reason to fear that they may some day have that effect.

Nor is *Lemon* to be taken as a retreat from *Walz*'s broader sanction, in dictum, of federal income exemptions which, since passage of the Sixteenth Amendment, have consistently been granted to eleemosynary groups as well as to corporations and associations organized and operated exclusively for religious purposes. Indeed, *Walz*'s longevity might have been divined from several auspices found in that case itself and in the composition of the Court which decided it.

For one, *Walz* itself had already thumbed the pages of history and had noted that in this country tax dispensations have been accorded churches "openly and by affirmative state action, not covertly or by state inaction," without interruption throughout our entire national and colonial existence and, while "no one acquires a vested or protected right in violation of the Constitution by long use,"

> Nothing in this national attitude toward religious tolerance and two centuries of uninterrupted freedom from taxation has given the remotest sign of leading to an established church or religion * * *. Thus, it is hardly useful to suggest that tax exemption is but the "foot in the door" or the "nose of the camel in the tent" leading to an established church. If tax exemption can be seen as this first step toward "establishment" of religion, as Mr. Justice Douglas fears, the second step has been long in coming. 397 U.S. at 678.

Indeed, the Court recalled the persuasive proverb of Mr. Justice Holmes, "If a thing has been practiced for two hundred years by common consent, it will need a strong case for the Fourteenth Amendment to affect it * * *." Jackman v. Rosenbaum Co., 260 U.S. 22, 31 (1922). To which we may add that the majority of the present Court, unlike that of the Warren Court, sees no stigma in being "among the last to lay the old aside."

Second, the Court's judgment in *Walz* provoked only one dissent, that of Justice Douglas. Third, it enjoyed the concurrence of Mr. Justice Brennan and Mr. Justice Marshall, two justices who exude sensitivity whenever they spy spots of potential Establishment in state or federal statutes. Finally, *Walz* was not a "parochial school case," that

[88]

sort of case which has repeatedly disturbed and divided the Court—see, e.g., the vigorous dissents in *Everson*, supra, as well as those in Board of Educ. v. Allen, supra, and note the splintering of the Court in other parochial school cases, infra § 2.02(n). It is safe to say that *Walz* remains accepted law today and reasonable to conclude that its rationale would justify federal and state income and excise tax exemptions.

In brief, though the significance of its tripartite test reached all areas of the Court's Establishment jurisprudence, *Lemon* was only a parochial school case. Its repercussions spread, however, far beyond the Catholic Church-related elementary and secondary schools. Not only did *Lemon* dictate the defeat of two carefully designed programs of aid for parochial schools, it also forecast fateful consequences for all other forms of financial aid for all other church-related elementary and secondary schools. Those consequences merit at least a summary enumeration.

Ever since *Everson* declared in 1947 that it "is much too late to argue that legislation intended to facilitate the opportunity of children to get a secular education serves no public purpose", argument persisted that the public purpose, which *Everson* found, rested not alone upon a legislative "child-safety" objective but alternatively and in equal measure upon a "child-secular education" cause. If that be true and if the parochial school provides, as it obviously does, a secular education, the inference extracted from *Everson* is that the parochial school's permeation of secular subjects with religious doctrine is really irrelevant. This "irrelevancy of permeation" thesis was, in fact, already moribund in 1971, the year of *Lemon*. And, if *Lemon*, with its portrait of the religiously permeated parochial school, did not address the issue directly, it did administer, sotto voce, last rites to the thesis.

In the context of *Lemon* and Earley v. DiCenso the "irrelevancy" argument presented several uncontroverted factual premises: each state had structured its financial aid programs to ensure the secular education of all its children; whether the secular education offered in church-related schools be immunized against religion or not, those schools possessed the competence to provide a secular education and the secular instruction offered each child therein did in fact satisfy state imposed educational standards; the quality of that secular education was no less than the quality of education in public schools, and the parochial school child's proficiency in secular subjects was at least equal to the proficiency of public school student; the statutory aid, both in *Lemon* and in Earley v. Di Censo, did not, and could not by its statutory terms, even approach the cost of the secular education services performed for the state in parochial schools or the cost of education in the state supported public schools. There was not, therefore, and there could not be, any surplus of state funds, thus exhausted in the compensation of a secular service rendered the state, which could come to the aid of the religious pursuits of the religious beneficiaries.

The secular appeal of church-related schools was not without merit. The student in the Yeshiva school learns that two and two are four the same as the student in the public school. In the Catholic parochial school the United States is bounded on the east by the Atlantic Ocean and on the west by the Pacific just as it is in the public school. And in the Lutheran school a plural subject requires a plural verb just as it does in the public school. From the point of view of the state's interest in secular education and its secular interest in unburdened budgets, the "irrelevancy" argument did present a realistic quid pro quo proposition, with the state getting the better of the bargain. This fiscal appeal carried with it a considerable equitable, and Constitutional, persuasion. It took account of Free Exercise considerations which caution against denial of financial aid for students in parochial schools only because in that environment they are being taught the tenets of the particular faith they are Constitutionally free to profess and to practice. And despite all that had been written about the permeated parochial schools, it was still possible to stress the secular in that environment, and soften the sectarian as only a secondary or ancillary function of those schools.

Indeed, the argument was given, *post hoc*, more than a semblance of support in Mr. Justice Powell's assertion, as a pre-*Lemon* principle, "Whatever may be its initial appeal, the proposition that the Establishment Clause prohibits any program which in some manner aids an institution with a religious affiliation has consistently been rejected. * * * Stated another way, the Court has not accepted the recurrent argument that all aid is forbidden because aid to one aspect of an institution frees it to spend its other resources on religious ends." Hunt v. McNair, 413 U.S. 734, 742–743 (1973).

If the "irrelevancy" or "ancillary" thesis were engendered by *Everson*'s recognition of the public or secular purpose served by parochial schools, it was, however, rather frail at birth. In *Everson* two issues were raised, the first under the Fourteenth Amendment's Due Process Clause per se and the second under the Establishment Clause. Mr. Justice Black addressed those issues in that order. He wrote of the "public purpose" served by church-related schools, and by all non-public schools, in answer to petitioner's pure Due Process claim, in answer to the contention that the state's reimbursement of transportation costs incurred by parents, who for personal reasons choose to send their children to "church schools," constituted a taking of taxpayers' private property for a private, non-public use. He did not write of a "public purpose" when he responded to petitioner's Estab-

[92]

lishment claim. In that second part of his opinion Justice Black spoke only of the very real hazards of traffic, of the state's interest in the safety and welfare of children and he concluded:

> This Court has said that parents may, in the discharge of their duty under state compulsory education laws, send their children to a religious rather than a public school if the school meets the secular educational requirements which the state has power to impose. See Pierce v. Society of Sisters, 268 U.S. 510. It appears that these parochial schools meet New Jersey's requirements. The State contributes no money to the schools. It does not support them. Its legislation, as applied, does no more than provide a general program to help parents get their children, regardless of their religion, safely and expeditiously to and from accredited schools. 330 U.S. at 18.

Thus, though the public service rendered by the parochial school may be a complete answer to a *per se* Due Process challenge to a state's spending of its tax receipts, it does not necessarily follow that the same service will satisfy the strictures of the Establishment Clause. The Fourteenth Amendment's Due Process Clause is in equipoise with the Establishment Clause only insofar as the Due Process clause incorporates the Establishment Clause and makes it applicable to the states.

The "irrelevancy" theme was also left rather limp by the implications in the *Everson* dictum, "No tax in any amount, large or small, can be levied to support any religious activities or institutions, whatever they may be called or whatever *form they may adopt to teach* or practice *religion*." 330 U.S. at 16. (Emphasis added). And, strangely enough, it would seem to have breathed its last in Board of Educ. v. Allen.

Though the *Allen* court sustained the loan of secular textbooks to students in parochial schools and though it underscored the dual function, secular and sectarian, served by those schools, it simply refused to conclude, on the record before it, that the processes of secular and religious training in parochial schools were so intertwined that secular textbooks furnished to students were *in fact* instrumental in teaching religion. Nothing in the record supported the proposition that all textbooks, whether they dealt, e.g., with mathematics, physics or history, were used by the parochial schools to teach religion. It is evident that, were they *in fact* so used, Mr. Justice White, in *Allen*, would have concluded that the textbook statute resulted in an "unconstitutional involvement of the State with religious instruction." 392 U.S. at 248, a position he confirmed in his separate opinion in the *Lemon* cases. See 403 U.S. at 666, 670–671.

Lemon was far more exacting than *Allen*. The latter required proof in fact of religious indoctrination. The former, posing a potential for infusion of secular subjects or secular teaching with sectarian doctrine, demanded that the state *insure* that subsidized teachers do not inculcate religion. Basically, it was only this actual versus potential by-play which produced the single dissent in the *Lemon* cases. There was unanimity in the Court's judgment that "permeation" is a very pertinent consideration. It is, in fact, a critical factor which requires, in the majority's view, no demonstration.

Lemon's demand for insurance against the blending of secular and sectarian education—a demand decreed by the Court after contemplation of its portrait of the parochial schools—created a dilemma for aid-inclined state legislatures and for the church-related elementary and secondary schools. It produced, in Mr. Justice White's words, "an insoluble paradox." He read in the Court's opinion an implicit conclusion that:

> The State cannot finance secular instruction if it permits religion to be taught in the same classroom; but if it exacts a promise that religion not be so taught—a promise the school and its teachers are quite willing and on this record able to give—and enforces it, it is then entangled in the "no entanglement" aspect of the Court's Establishment Clause jurisprudence. 403 U.S. at 668. (White J., concurring in part and dissenting in part).

The majority opinion did not expressly proscribe, on pain of forfeiture of state financial aid, the teaching of religion and secular subjects "in the same classroom." What it did proscribe was the use of state financed secular instruction for the inculcation of religion, and it found a potential for such misuse. Thus stated, though, the riddle remains and for programs in aid of parochial schools it poses the inescapable alternatives of condemnation under the non-secular effect test of Establishment or invalidity under the non-entanglement principle. Norwood v. Harrison, 413 U.S. 455, 468 (1973), noted that escape is possible, that we can insulate the religious instruction from the secular education of the parochial schools. And *Allen* actually accomplished that feat. Yet, reconciliation of *Allen* with *Lemon* also presents a paradox of sorts. *Allen*, however, as noted below, has been twice reaffirmed. But, perforce of *Lemon*, it just about marks the boundary line for ideological aid to church-related elementary and secondary schools.

The *Lemon-DiCenso* profile of a parochial school, with its potential for permeation, was laminated and exhibited—albeit on uncontroverted allegations or specific findings made by a district court in each instance—in later cases to fault, per se, various forms of aid to church-related schools. See, e.g., Levitt v. Committee for Public Educ., 413 U.S. 472 (1973); Committee for Public Educ. v.

Nyquist, 413 U.S. 756 (1973) and cases noted infra, § 2.04(c).

But first, as to the profile itself, quite apart from its self-contained capacity to bar all meaningful governmental aid for parochial schools, one may wonder, at this juncture, whether it is valid to cast all church-related schools in the image of a Catholic church-related school. Neither in Rhode Island nor in Pennsylvania were Roman Catholic schools singled out for assistance. They simply existed and operated in a class of non-public schools to which, or to whose secular teachers, financial assistance was sought to be given. There are non-sectarian private schools within that category as well as Jewish, Lutheran, Episcopal, Seventh Day Adventist and other church-affiliated schools.

It may well be that neither the Court's portrait of the two parochial school systems before it in *Lemon* nor Mr. Justice Douglas' detailed delineation of the religious character of Rhode Island's Roman Catholic schools captures the complete features of the Yeshiva, the Lutheran school or other church-related schools. Perhaps it is palpably evident that "the characteristics of individual schools may vary widely from that profile." Committee for Public Educ. v. Nyquist, supra, 413 U.S. at 768. But, the *Nyquist* Court did not seek to ascertain in what essential respects, if any, other schools may "vary widely" from Roman Catholic parochial schools. It proceeded directly to an evaluation of the merits of the case and invalidated for all church-related schools the three financial aid programs for nonpublic elementary and secondary schools therein challenged.

Whatever differing features, presumably incidental, may be found in sectarian schools of other faiths, it is evident today that the die has been cast and it impresses upon every church-related school the *Lemon*-like profile of the Catholic parochial school with its potential for permeating secular subjects and secular instruction with sectarian indoctrination. It is as though the Court, having condemned as governmental entanglement with religious institutions any "comprehensive, discriminating and continuing surveillance" of the parochial school's religious teaching, refused itself to become entangled in the evaluation of the religious content, the proselytizing mission or the propagative purpose of one parochial school of a particular religious faith vis-a-vis that of another religious faith.

No record was developed in the *Nyquist* case. The district court, "relying on findings in a similar case recently decided by the same court, adopted a profile of these sectarian, nonpublic schools similar to the one suggested in plaintiffs' complaint." Mr. Justice Powell, writing for the Court, stated that "[q]ualifying institutions, under all three segments of the [challenged] enactment, *could be*

ones" described by the profile. 413 U.S. at 767.
(Emphasis added). Recognizing, as we obviously
must, that the profile could not possibly characterize the non-sectarian nonpublic schools, which were
also beneficiaries of New York's legislative programs, the "could be" verbalization was ominous
for them as well. In *Nyquist* no argument was
made that the statutory aid should survive for the
private non-sectarian schools or, for that matter,
for those parochial schools which "vary widely"
from the adopted profile. The argument was prof-
fered in Sloan v. Lemon, 413 U.S. 825 (1973), and
there embellished with a bootstrap Equal Protection claim. Mr. Justice Powell reserved for that
case clarification of the "could be" predicate he
used in *Nyquist*. He wrote in *Sloan*:

> Apart from the Establishment Clause issues
> central to this case, appellant-intervenors
> * * * make an equal protection claim that was
> not directly ruled on by the District Court.
> These intervenors are 12 parents whose chil-
> dren attend nonpublic schools. Two parents
> * * * send their child to a nonsectarian
> school while the remainder send their children
> to sectarian schools. The District Court's final
> order enjoined the State Treasurer from dis-
> bursing funds to any parents, irrespective of
> whether their children attended sectarian or
> nonsectarian schools. The court considered
> and rejected the argument that the state law

should be treated "as containing a separable provision for aid to parents of children attending nonpublic schools that are not church related." Although the Act contained a severability clause, the court reasoned that, in view of the fact that so substantial a majority of the law's designated beneficiaries were affiliated with religious organizations, it could not be assumed that the state legislature would have passed the law to aid only those attending the relatively few nonsectarian schools.

Appellants ask this Court to declare the provisions severable and thereby to allow tuition reimbursement for parents of children attending schools that are not church related. If the parents of children who attend nonsectarian schools receive assistance, their argument continues, parents of children who attend sectarian schools are entitled to the same aid as a matter of equal protection. The argument is thoroughly spurious. In the first place, we have been shown no reason to upset the District Court's conclusion that aid to the nonsectarian school could not be severed from aid to the sectarian. The statute nowhere sets up this suggested dichotomy between sectarian and nonsectarian schools, and to approve such a distinction here would be to create a program quite different from the one the legislature actually adopted. * * * Even if the Act were clearly severable, valid aid to nonpublic, nonsectarian schools would provide no lever for aid to their sectarian counterparts. The Equal Protection Clause has never been regarded as a bludgeon with which to compel a State to violate other provisions of the Constitution. Having held that tuition reimbursements for the benefit of sectarian schools violate the Establishment Clause, nothing in the Equal Protection Clause will suffice to revive that program. 413 U.S. at 833–834.

Mr. Justice Powell's response revealed political acumen as well as Constitutional common sense. Simple statistics verify the numerical predominance of Catholic parochial schools over private non-sectarian elementary and secondary schools. The statistics almost compel the conclusion that acceptance of the suggested dichotomy between sectarian and non-sectarian schools would indeed create "a program quite different from the one the legislature actually adopted." The same statistics suggest that a distinction between Catholic parochial schools and other sectarian schools would also produce a program quite different from the one the legislature proposed.

It will be recalled from *Lemon* that all of the 250 Rhode Island teachers who had applied for benefits under the Rhode Island act were employed by Roman Catholic schools. In 1971, the year of

Lemon, Rhode Island's nonpublic elementary schools accommodated approximately 25% of that state's pupils and 95% of those pupils attended schools affiliated with the Roman Catholic church. More than 96% of the 535,215 pupils in Pennsylvania's recipient nonpublic schools attended church-related schools and most of those schools were affiliated with the Roman Catholic church. 403 U.S. at 608, 610. In the fall of 1968 there were 2,038 nonpublic schools in New York State: 1,415 Roman Catholic; 164 Jewish; 59 Lutheran; 49 Episcopal; 37 Seventh Day Adventist; 18 other church affiliated; and 296 without religious affiliation. Committee for Public Educ. v. Nyquist, 413 U.S. at 768, n.23. During the 1974–1975 school year, of the 720 chartered nonpublic schools in Ohio all but 29 were sectarian. More than 96% of the nonpublic enrollment attended sectarian schools and more than 92% attended Catholic schools. Wolman v. Walter, 433 U.S. 229, 234 (1977). These statistics are taken from localized areas but they have a near national significance. And, though nonpublic school enrollments have declined in recent years and the financial insecurity of private schools is predictive of a continuing declension, the overall pattern remains substantially the same. See *Nyquist*, 413 U.S. at 816–818 (White, J., dissenting).

In the face of these statistics, in this particularly sensitive legislative area, it would be rather naive to expect that any legislature would propose a partitioning of nonpublic schools that might result in aid to non-sectarian schools but denial of aid to the church-related sector, or which might conceivably produce aid, e. g., to Mormon schools but deny it to those of other faiths. One would think that only a politically mindless legislator (which may well be a contradiction in terms) would risk a vote in favor of an explicit and unequivocal severability clause. It is, very simply stated, not politically feasible.

This preclusion of state financial aid for non-sectarian nonpublic schools is not the final illustration of *Lemon*'s impact. The rapid succession of cases which followed upon *Lemon* are summarized in § 2.04. In practice *Lemon*'s Establishment jurisprudence grew distended and was applied pervasively, apparently far beyond the expectations of its creator. Four years after *Lemon*, Chief Justice Burger was to reject the Court's "extravagant suggestion of potential entanglement" found to inhere in another Pennsylvania program of financial aid, one which provided "auxiliary services," such as counseling, testing, psychological assistance, etc., to parochial school students. Meek v. Pittenger, 421 U.S. 349, 385 (1975). (Burger, C. J., concurring in part and dissenting in part). Burger, C. J., may have wondered what hath the Chief Justice wrought in *Lemon*. Whether it be hope or hopelessness which springs eternal for parochial schools, and for all private elementary and secondary schools, Chief Justice Burger himself could "only hope that, at some future date, the Court will come to a more enlightened and tolerant view of the First Amendment's guarantee of free exercise of religion, thus eliminating the denial of equal protection to children in church-sponsored schools, and take a more realistic view that carefully limited aid to children is not a step toward establishing a state religion—at least while this Court sits." 421 U.S. at 387.

(n) The Present Status of the Tripartite Test—Its Incongruous Applications

We have already noted that *Lemon*'s initial significance, and doctrinally its overriding significance, lay in its explicit enunciation of the tripartite test. In *Lemon* the test was accepted by a seven judge majority of the Court, with only Justice White's "insoluble paradox" casting its solitary shadow on the non-entanglement principle. In neither of the two separate concurring opinions, that of Justice Douglas (who also joined in the opinion of the Court) and that of Justice Brennan (who did not), was any issue taken respecting the test itself.

Justice Douglas, it can be said, had never found any particular virtue in silence. He wrote his concurrence in *Lemon*, to invigorate, it seems, the Court's Establishment tests, to provide an accompanying fortissimo for the Court's "legalistic minuet," or what Chief Justice Burger, with artistic ambiguity, styled a "true minuet" which is "a matter of pure form and style, the observance of which is itself the substantive end." 403 U.S. at 614. Quoting from *Walz*, "We must also be sure that the end result—the effect—is not excessive government entanglement with religion", Justice Douglas concluded, "There is in my view such an entanglement here" and he stated specifically, "Whatever may be the result in case of grants to students, it is clear that once one of the States finances a private school, it is duty-bound to make certain that the school stays within secular bounds and does not use the public funds to promote sectarian causes." 403 U.S. at 627, 632–633.

Mr. Justice Brennan, reiterated his personal three pronged formulation, first set forth in his Abington School Dist. v. Schempp concurrence, that the Establishment Clause forbids "those involvements of religious with secular institutions which (a) serve the essentially religious activities of religious institutions; (b) employ the organs of government for essentially religious purposes; or (c) use essentially religious means to serve governmental ends, where secular means would suffice." 403 U.S. at 643.

The three-tiered—secular purpose, secular effect, non-entanglement—test also found favor with a majority of the Court in Tilton v. Richardson, 403 U.S. 672 (1971), which was announced the same day as Lemon v. Kurtzman. While Chief Justice Burger's opinion, there applying the tripartite test to sustain federal financial aid for church-related colleges, enjoyed the complete concurrence of only Justices Harlan, Stewart and Blackmun, Mr. Justice Douglas, with whom Justices Black and Marshall joined, concurring in part and dissenting in part, adopted the same test—or a reasonable facsimile thereof—to invalidate the federal grants in toto.

Justice Douglas acknowledged the public purpose but refused to accept either its secular effect or the absence of an inevitable, and Constitutionally inescapable, entanglement. He wrote:

> The public purpose in secular education is, to be sure, furthered by the program. Yet the sectarian purpose is aided by making the parochial school system viable. * * *

> The facilities financed by taxpayers' funds are not to be used for "sectarian" purposes. Religious teaching and secular teaching are so enmeshed in parochial schools that only the strictest supervision and surveillance would insure compliance with the condition.

> * * *

> In other words, surveillance creates an entanglement of government and religion which the First Amendment was designed to avoid. 403 U.S. at 692–694.

Justice Douglas echoed here his *Lemon* concurrence. Rather than disparage the tripartite test, he demanded a consistent, and scrupulously strict application thereof. His profile of the parochial school was a stereotype which left its imprint upon university education as well as the grammar grades. He simply refused to distinguish church-related colleges from church-related elementary or secondary schools.

Though the Supreme Court normally moves with glacial speed, it proceeded expeditiously in 1973 to consideration of five school cases. They were Committee for Public Educ. v. Nyquist, supra; Levitt v. Committee for Public Educ., supra; Sloan v. Lemon, supra; Hunt v. McNair, supra; and Norwood v. Harrison, supra. In all of these the tripartite guidelines were confirmed and in all with the blessings of a majority of the Court. Two years later the tests again found favor with a majority in Meek v. Pittenger, 421 U.S. 349 (1975). But, only a year after *Meek* a sort of exorcism of tripartitism was performed by Justices White and Rehnquist. It came in the former's concurring opinion (joined in by the latter) in Roemer v. Maryland Public Works Bd., 426 U.S. 736, 767 (1976) with the result, it has been said, that the test ultimately lost its majority status in Wolman v. Walter, supra. If this is so, then the Establishment principles of the individual Justices might well be in a class with Mr. Justice Roberts' "restricted railroad ticket, good for this day and train only." Smith v. Allwright, 321 U.S. 649, 669 (1944) (Roberts, J., dissenting). But, it is not so—not precisely so. A brief consideration of *Roemer* and *Wolman* is appropriate.

Roemer was a variation on the *Tilton* theme which sustained federal aid to "parochial colleges," as Mr. Justice Douglas was wont to characterize church-related institutions of higher education. The 5 to 4 decision, accepting a broader range of college grants than had been approved in *Tilton*, produced five separate opinions. Mr. Justice Blackmun, joined by the Chief Justice and Justice Powell, adhered to the tripartite analysis. Justice White, with whom Mr. Justice Rehnquist joined, concurred in the Court's judgment but he, whose "insoluble paradox" had sounded an alarm against the non-entanglement element, could not be reconciled to *Lemon*'s threefold test. As long as there was a secular legislative purpose, and as long as the primary effect of the legislation was neither to advance nor inhibit religion, there was for him no cause "to take the constitutional inquiry further." The same factors, he argued, upon which the plurality focused in concluding that the legislation satisfied the second part of the *Lemon* test, were repeated to absolve the state of any excessive entanglement with religion. He saw no reason "to indulge in the redundant exercise of evaluating the same facts and findings under a different label."

What Justice White considered superfluous Justice Brennan (with whom Justice Marshall joined) and Justice Stevens, in separate dissents, considered critical. Mr. Justice Brennan repeated his consistent position that general· subsidies of religious activities constitute "impermissible state involvement with religion," a "necessarily deep involvement of government * * * through the policing of restrictions." It is entanglement which is anathema but entanglement here was the product of the "effect" infirmity which inhered in the state legislation. For, in the Brennan view, when a state subsidizes an institution dedicated to two goals, secular education and religious instruction, both functions benefit from those subsidies. The reasoning does suggest that "effect" and "entanglement" are one and it has that ring of redundancy to which Justice White objected. But, Mr. Justice Brennan did not consider it redundant to add that "[t]he discrete interests of government and religion are mutually best served when each avoids too close a proximity with the other." 426 U.S. at 772.

This popular appeal to the best interests of religion caught Mr. Justice Stevens' fancy, as did Justice Brennan's adamantine antipathy to potential entanglement. Justice Stevens wrote a short paragraph to emphasize "the pernicious tendency of a state subsidy to tempt religious schools to compromise their religious mission without wholly abandoning it. The disease of entanglement may infect a law discouraging wholesome religious activity as well as a law encouraging the propagation of a given faith." 426 U.S. at 775. Justice Stevens apparently sought to sweeten adversity but it was an ironic twist, this protective counselling that entanglement "may infect a law discouraging wholesome religious activity." Recognizing the varied and on-going programs of financial aid for parochial schools devised by state legislatures over the last ten years, one would suspect that those schools would surely love to be tempted "to compromise their religious mission without wholly abandoning it."

Mr. Justice Stewart was *Roemer*'s remaining dissenter. He concluded that "[i]n the present case by contrast [with *Tilton*], the compulsory theology courses may be 'devoted to deepening religious experiences in the particular faith rather than to teaching theology as an academic discipline' [thereby exposing] 'State money for use in advancing religion, no matter the vigilance to avoid it.'" 426 U.S. at 774-775. He found a non-secular effect in the Maryland subsidies and it was, therefore, unnecessary to examine the entanglement side of the triangle. Thus, he did not contest the tripartite test. Indeed, he accepted it in Wolman v. Walter, supra, wherein he joined in the plurality opinion which expressly adhered to the purpose —effect—non-entanglement analysis.

On the other hand, if Mr. Justice Stevens could be said to have accepted the non-entanglement principle in *Roemer*, he abandoned it in *Wolman* with a simple footnote observation that "[i]t is the sectarian school itself, not the legislation, that is 'entangled' with religion." He renounced the tripartite test itself as an unsuccessful effort to improve upon the *Everson* dictum that "a state subsidy of sectarian schools is invalid regardless of the form it takes." 433 U.S. at 265.

Wolman presented a challenge to an Ohio statute which authorized the State to provide elementary and secondary nonpublic school pupils with secular textbooks, standardized testing and scoring services, diagnostic and therapeutic services, instructional materials and equipment, and field trip services. Mr. Justice Blackmun announced the judgment of the Court and an opinion in Part II whereof he reiterated *Lemon*'s three part test. In addition to Mr. Justice Stewart, that segment of his opinion had the concurrence of the Chief Justice and Mr. Justice Powell. In that part, it was, as noted, only a plurality opinion but again the separate opinion of Mr. Justice Brennan and that of Mr. Justice Marshall must be considered if we are to resist the conclusion that tripartitism has lost its majority status or its effectiveness.

Both Justice Brennan and Justice Marshall emphasized "the divisive political potential" of Ohio's program of aid to sectarian schools as one of the dangers of entanglement. Mr. Justice Brennan found the Ohio programs unconstitutional in their entirety. He would have invalidated those programs which the Court held to have avoided "an effect or entanglement condemned by the Establishment Clause." He argued that "ingenuity in draftsmanship cannot obscure the fact that this subsidy to sectarian schools amounts to $88,800,000 * * * just for the initial biennium" and evaluation of this factor "compels * * * the conclusion that a divisive political potential of unusual magnitude inheres in the Ohio program." 433 U.S. at 256. Mr. Justice Marshall expressed the same view and repeated *Lemon*'s concern "with the danger that the need for annual appropriations of larger and larger sums would lead to '[p]olitical fragmentation and divisiveness on religious lines.'" 433 U.S. at 258.

Thus, while Justices White and Rehnquist demand proof of a secular purpose and a secular effect, the first two parts of the *Lemon* trilogy, and look askance at "political divisiveness" and consider other aspects of entanglement tautological, Justices Brennan and Marshall, for whom "divisiveness" is the deadly evil of an Establishment, would condemn any legislation which has a tendency to induce "political divisiveness" among the various religious faiths. What can be extracted from the individual opinions of the Justices is a majority consensus that all three parts of the test, howsoever each Justice may define or refine each separate part, must be satisfied if legislation or governmental practices are to escape Constitutional condemnation. Certainly, to that very practical extent tripartitism is still operative and has maintained its majority status. Indeed, in form as well as in effect, the test was reaccepted in the Court's 5-4 decision in Committee for Public Educ. v. Regan, 444 U.S. 646 (1980). Writing for the majority, Justice White applied the tripartite test "under the precedents of this Court", while Justice Blackmun, with whom Justices Brennan and Marshall joined in dissent, agreed that the "mode of analysis for Establishment Clause questions is defined by the three-part test that has emerged from the Court's decisions."

That is not at all to suggest that the test has produced coherence in the Court's Establishment Clause judgments, nor to suggest that it is an historically accurate statement of what those who proposed and who ratified the First Amendment really intended, or even an acceptably logical inference from what they said or wrote elsewhere on the subject of government and religion. Though the Court, at least in this century, has never placed consistency among the more exalted virtues, the three part test, articulated as a concise and clear rationalization of prior Establishment Clause adjudications, raised expectations that it would promote an harmonious process for the resolution of Establishment issue yet to come. It has yet to achieve that non-virtuous objective.

The test was first fully formulated in Lemon v. Kurtzman. Mr. Justice White found *Lemon* itself inherently paradoxical. It has to date produced, particularly in the parochial school cases, more paradoxes than ever perplexed the mind of Mr. Pond. Mr. Justice White is consigned to live in a wonderland of paradox. Lawyer and layman alike must have been wondrously perplexed when the Court told us that the state would be compelled to police the teaching of the partially subsidized secular instructor in the church-affiliated elementary and secondary schools, although surveillance is not mandated to guard against indoctrination by the religiously-inspired teacher in the wholly funded public school; that the state may lend text books to parochial school students but that it may not lend those same students, or their parents, movie projectors, tape recorders, record players, maps and globes, science kits or weather forecasting charts; that a state may exempt church property from taxation but that it may not provide state income tax credits or income tax deductions for parents who pay tuition to church-related elementary and secondary schools; that the state may provide free bus transportation, to and from school, for children attending parochial schools but it may not provide the same transportation for the same students for trips to governmental, industrial, cultural and scientific centers designed to enrich their secular studies; that the state may provide direct, noncategorical funding of church-related colleges, but may not provide indirect, and restricted financial assistance for church-affiliated secondary schools; that the state may not provide, for children with special needs, remedial and accelerated instruction, guidance counseling and testing, speech and hearing services, on nonpublic school premises, but that it may provide speech and hearing diagnostic services in the nonpublic school; and that the state may provide—in public schools, public centers or mobile units—therapeutic services for deaf, blind, emotionally disturbed, crippled and physically handicapped nonpublic school children but that it may not provide the same services for the same children on the nonpublic school premises.

If *Lemon* itself were a curiosity, its subsequent applications, thus summarized, have grown "curiouser and curiouser". And yet it is a very specific test, very simply stated: secular purpose, secular effect, non-entanglement. Though one might sensibly argue that the Court states no more than a conclusion without justifying it when it declares that an enactment having the purpose and effect of aiding religion is an Establishment of Religion, the two pronged test put together in Abington School Dist. v. Schempp in 1963 was an adequate synthesis of a previously unarticulated rationale, and of the result reached, in the cases from Bradfield v. Roberts in 1899 down to Engel v.

Vitale in 1962. The holdings in almost all of those cases were sought, however, to be justified by readings of history which were consistently challenged for their lack of scholarship. *Walz*, in fashioning its non-entanglement principle, sought to give a rule of reason to sustain church tax exemptions. It succeeded, and did so with a majority concurrence. But, the non-entanglement standard itself sprouted several branches in Lemon v. Kurtzman some of which find no firming roots either in history or in reason.

So, while the tripartite test is a noble effort to achieve uniformity, and a concise exposition of results to be achieved, the fact remains that unanimous acceptance of the tripartite test would not produce unanimity in results. That is so because each justice is necessarily left to his own sense of history, his own rules of logic, his own notions of *stare decisis* and perhaps, as Mr. Justice Jackson put it, his own "prepossessions" to define and apply the terms of the test. The principles, particularly "effect" and "entanglement," are more easily stated than they are applied. There is no doubt that in any given case the tripartite standard can be refined and used to sustain aid to religious institutions or to condemn it.

From the cumulative criteria developed by the Court, however, we can formulate, if not absolutes, at least some guides for ascertaining what constitutes a secular legislative purpose, what produces a principal or primary effect which neither advances nor inhibits religion and what escapes an excessive governmental entanglement with religion.

§ 2.03 A Secular Legislative Purpose

Mr. Justice Stone once wrote, "Inquiry into the hidden motives which may move Congress to exercise a power constitutionally conferred upon it is beyond the competency of courts." Sonzinsky v. United States, 300 U.S. 506 (1937). Indeed, it is not within the province of the Court to psychoanalyze any legislature, state or federal. With the possible exception of Epperson v. Arkansas, 393 U.S. 97 (1968), discussed below, the Court has been faithful to that principle in applying the Establishment test—even though a secular legislative "purpose" is expressly stated as the first tier thereof. This is simply to say that "purpose" is something to be found on the face of the statute, in its preamble or in legislative declarations.

When a non-religious purpose is recited "the stated legislative intent * * * must therefore be accorded appropriate deference." Lemon v. Kurtzman, supra, 403 U.S. at 613. To this principle, too, the Court has been faithful. It has been most respectfully faithful. For, in practice the Court has been equally deferential to mere indicia of a non-religious purpose found in the statute itself or extracted from its legislative history. As a consequence the "secular legislative purpose" requirement has been the least controversial part of the tripartite test. It has provoked very little judicial debate and none of particular significance.

A secular legislative purpose was readily found in all the parochial school cases and in the three church-related college cases, Tilton v. Richardson, Hunt v. McNair, and Roemer v. Maryland Public Works Bd. And in no case since *Epperson* has it been suggested that the legislative purpose might have been an exclusively religious one. It would not be improper to conclude, but again with *Epperson* aside, that when a statute can be said to be plausibly, or even colorably, non-religious, it is sufficiently secular in purpose.

This rule-of-thumb is a reasonable inference from those cases which came after Abington School Dist. v. Schempp. And it sits comfortably with those which pre-dated *Schempp*'s formulation of the secular purpose—secular effect standard. The comfortable posture of the purpose prerequisite in the pre-*Schempp* cases is evident in *Everson* and evident as well in McGowan v. Maryland, 366 U.S. 420 (1961). And, despite several contrary implications to be found in Gillette v. United States, 401 U.S. 437 (1971), the casual disposition of the Establishment Clause contention in Arver v. United States might also be put at ease.

Mr. Justice Black wrote of New Jersey's legislative "purpose" in the Due Process part of his *Everson* opinion and he noted no difficulty in ascertaining it. Recognizing that "church schools" provide a secular, as well as a religious, education for their students, he found as a fact, as did the New Jersey Court of Errors and Appeals below, that "the New Jersey legislature has decided that a public purpose was served by using tax-raised funds to pay the bus fares of all school children, including those who attend parochial schools." It was, he said, "much too late to argue that legislation *intended* to facilitate the opportunity of children to get a secular education serves no public purpose" and the same conclusion was "no less true of legislation to reimburse needy parents, or all parents, for payment of the fares of their children so that they can ride in public buses to and from schools rather than run the risk of traffic and other hazards incident to walking or 'hitchhiking' ". 330 U.S. at 3, 6–7. (Emphasis added). While bus transportation to and from school is not designed to improve the quality of secular education in sectarian schools, most certainly the Court today, given the obvious child-safety interest, would not, and rationally could not, if deference be due to the state legislature, impute a religious or non-secular motivation to the New Jersey Legislature or to the Ewing Township Board of Education.

In his search for a secular legislative purpose Mr. Chief Justice Warren wrote at greater length in McGowan v. Maryland than did Justice Black in *Everson*—and not by reason of Warren's love of language. *McGowan* was the Sunday closing case and Sunday closing laws were in origin undeniably dictated by religious motivations.

Margaret McGowan and her fellow petitioners, employees of a discount department store in Maryland, were convicted in a Maryland state court of selling on a Sunday a loose-leaf binder, a can of floor wax, a stapler, staples and a toy, in violation of a Maryland statute which prohibited the sale on Sunday of all merchandise except specified health and recreation related commodities. Appellants offered Equal Protection, Establishment Clause and Free Exercise objections. The essence of appellants' Establishment argument centered on the fact that Sunday is the Sabbath day of the predominant religious sects and on the allegation that the purpose of the enforced stoppage of labor on that day was, and is, to facilitate and to encourage church attendance. Chief Justice Warren, in an opinion which five other members of the Court joined, sustained the Maryland statute. He acknowledged that the original laws, in Maryland and in other states, which dealt with Sunday labor "were motivated by religious forces." But, "what we must decide", he said, "is whether the present Sunday legislation, having undergone extensive changes from the earliest forms, still retains its religious character." 366 U.S. at 431.

The Chief Justice retraced the history of Sunday laws from the edict of Henry III in 1237, which forbade the frequenting of markets on Sunday; to the statute of 29 Charles II in 1677, which prohibited "any worldly business or work" on Sunday so that all might better observe "the Lord's day" by "repairing to church thereon"; and into the statutes of early colonial times, in the Plymouth Colony, the Massachusetts Bay Colony, the Connecticut and New Haven Colonies and in Maryland itself, captioned as laws "concerning Religion" and enacted "to the end the Sabbath may be celebrated in a religious manner." Royal proclamations, acts of parliament, colonial statutes, all glistened with pure religious motivations.

As early as 1750, however, Sunday laws began to cast a secular glow. In the mid-18th century Blackstone was able to state that the keeping of "one day in seven holy, as a time of relaxation and refreshment as well as for public worship, is of admirable service to a state considered merely as a civil institution * * * it enables the industrious workman to pursue his occupation in the ensuing week with health and cheerfulness." And with the advent of the First Amendment, colonial provisions requiring church attendance vanished. The concept of a day of rest and recreation remained, however, and it found support in wholly secular circles in England and in most of the States of the United States where Sunday laws were espoused by labor groups and trade associations. Chief Justice Warren ultimately found his way out of history's Sunday-closed corridors to confront in the light of the present day the present Maryland statutes, the specific statutes before the Court in *McGowan.*

Though one section of the existing Maryland laws characterized Sunday as "the Lord's day" and suffered none "to profane the Lord's day," the statutes taken in their entirety "were not simply verbatim re-enactments of their religiously oriented antecedents." As a whole the various statutes presented salutary secular credentials. The sale of tobacco, of alcoholic beverages and a long list of sundry articles was permitted; the operation of bathing beaches and amusement parks and even the playing of pinball machines and slot machines —activities condemned in earlier religiously rooted legislation—were not forbidden; nor were shops with only one employee required to close on Sunday. These provisions, enhanced by those which permitted various sports and entertainment on Sunday, seemed "clearly to be fashioned for the purpose of providing a Sunday atmosphere of recreation, cheerfulness, repose and enjoyment" and a day of "relaxation rather than religion." Having engaged "in the close scrutiny demanded * * * when First Amendment liberties are at issue," Chief Justice Warren, with a deferential nod for the Maryland Court of Appeals, concluded that the statute's present purpose was not to aid religion but "to set aside a day of rest and recreation."

In Arver v. United States the Court, in 1917 admittedly not the activist First Amendment Court it is today, had considered scrutiny superfluous. *Arver* summarily dismissed an Establishment challenge to those provisions of the Selective Draft Act of 1917 which exempted ministers and divinity students from military service and which relieved from combat duty "conscientious objectors" who belonged to "any well-recognized religious sect or organization * * * whose existing creed or principles forbid its members to participate in war in any form and whose religious convictions are against war or participation therein." Subjected to a *McGowan*-like scrutiny, both the exemption of clerics and seminarians and the non-combatant classification accorded religious conscientious objectors might very well reflect a secular legislative purpose. Both may reflect a purely practical judgment by Congress that religious objectors, however admirable, proficient and patriotic they may be, are of "no more use in combat than many others unqualified for military service" and that the military is best served by those who are prepared "to undertake the fighting that the armed forces have to do." Welsh v. United States, 398 U.S. 333 (1970) (White, J., dissenting)—a secular motivation forcefully paraphrased by Mr. Justice Marshall as a pragmatic recognition by Congress of "the hopelessness of converting a sincere conscientious objector into an effective fighting man." Gillette v. United States, 401 U.S. at 453.

Historically, exemption of clergy and seminarians from military service has long been accepted without Constitutional qualms. Conscientious objector statutes, equally as venerable, have also been accepted but, in more recent periods of conscription, not without challenge. In 1775 the Continental Congress declared its resolve to respect the beliefs of "people who from Religious Principles cannot bear Arms in any case." *Gillette*, 401 U.S. at 443–444, n.8. From the first federal Draft Act of 1864 and through all subsequent selective service statutes the Congress of the United States has accorded similar respect to those who professed sincere religious scruples against service in the armed forces. Exemptions either from combat service or from all military service were fixed in terms of "religious" training or beliefs. The "religious" line of demarcation presented a Constitutional issue of more substance than *Arver* was willing to admit. In the interim between *Arver* and *Gillette* the Court managed, however, by a remarkable feat of statutory construction, to translate the Congressional "religious" test into secular terms and thereby avoided the Constitutional question.

The Draft Act of 1917 extended exemption only to those conscientious objectors affiliated with a "well-recognized religious sect or organization." The disparate treatment of religious sects apparently broke down in administrative practice by reason of the impracticability of compiling a list of "recognized" sects, Welsh v. United States, 398 U.S. at 367, n. 19. (Harlan, J., concurring). It did not appear in subsequent conscription statutes. The Selective Service Act of 1948 limited conscientious objector status to those who, "by reason of religious training and belief [are] conscientiously opposed to participation in war." The statute carefully defined "religious training and belief" as "an individual's belief in a relation to a Supreme Being involving duties superior to those arising from any human relation," but not including "essentially political, sociological or philosophical views or a merely personal moral code." 62 Stat. 612. Confronted with an Establishment Clause challenge, an unanimous Court with exceptional surgical expertise performed a resection to cure the statute of its asserted Constitutional infirmity. It construed the explicit statutory test of a belief "in relation to a Supreme Being" to encompass any sincere belief which occupies in the life of its possessor a place parallel to that which an orthodox belief in God occupies in the life of the orthodox believer. United States v. Seeger, 380 U.S. 163 (1965).

After a 1967 amendment deleted the reference to a "Supreme Being" but continued the provision that "religious training and belief" does not include "essentially political, sociological or philosophical views, or a merely personal moral code," a plurality of four Justices, in Welsh v. United States, again sidestepped the Constitutional issue by construing the religious requirement to include moral, ethical, religious beliefs about what is right or wrong. A registrant's characterization of his belief as "nonreligious," Mr. Justice Black wrote for the plurality, was a "highly unreliable guide" for determining conscientious objector status. Mr. Justice Harlan concurred on Constitutional grounds. He rejected the plurality's construction of the statutory test as contrary to its intended meaning and he found the statute incompatible with the Establishment Clause because it drew a non-neutral exemption line "between theistic or nontheistic religious beliefs on the one hand and secular beliefs on the other." The dissent of Mr. Justice White, which had the concurrence of Chief Justice Burger and Justice Stewart, accepted Harlan's understanding of the statute but rejected the Constitutional challenge.

These artful evasions of Constitutional questions ended with Gillette v. United States. In *Gillette* the Court confronted full face an Establishment Clause challenge, of only a slightly different stripe, and sustained the statute as written by Congress. Unfortunately, however, the majority opinion of Mr. Justice Marshall is not one of his more lucid opinions.

The challenged provision, § 6(j) of the Military Service Act of 1967, limited conscientious objector status to those who, by reason of religious training and belief, were conscientiously opposed to participation in "war in any form," i. e., to those who are opposed to all wars and not to those who are opposed to a particular war only—even though the latter objection "may have such roots in a claimant's conscience * * * that it is 'religious' in character." Petitioners' "religious" convictions did not dictate opposition to all wars but only to an "unjust" war, which they assessed the Vietnam conflict to be. No question was raised respecting the sincerity or the religious quality of their claims.

Justice Marshall frankly acknowledged that there are "religious" objectors who are not opposed to all wars but only to particular wars. He acknowledged that Section 6(j), properly construed, did have the effect of denying petitioners' claims to relief while accepting other "religious" claims—a de facto discrimination among religious and a potentially impermissible preference for some religious objectors over other religious objectors.

He restated *Schempp*'s secular purpose—secular effect test and while he expressly subscribed to that two tier standard, he seemed to speak almost exclusively of the secular purpose and very little of the primary effect. He seemed to hold that the alleged discrimination must appear *on the face* of the challenged statute.

> The critical weakness of petitioners' estab-
> lishment claim arises from the fact that § 6
> (j), on its face, simply does not discriminate on
> the basis of religious affiliation or religious
> belief, apart of course from beliefs concerning
> war. The section says that anyone who is
> conscientiously opposed to all war shall be re-
> lieved of military service. The specified objec-
> tion must have a grounding in "religious train-
> ing and belief," but no particular sectarian af-
> filiation or theological position is required.
> 401 U.S. at 450–451.

He added that a claimant alleging "gerrymander"
must be able to show "the absence of a neutral,
secular basis for the lines government has drawn."
The facial absence of any disparate disposition of
religious claims or religious beliefs did not, however, end inquiry. Justice Marshall stated affirmatively that Section 6(j) served "a number of
valid purposes having nothing to do with a design
to foster or favor any sect, religion or cluster of
religions."

The hopelessness of converting a sincere conscientious objector into an efficient fighting man,
noted above, is on its face certainly a secular concern but it goes to support the existence of an
exemption rather than its restriction to persons
who object to all wars. Yet, as to the latter restriction, there were, in that "number of valid
purposes having nothing to do with a design" to

discriminate among religions or religious claims, two overriding neutral legislative objectives: first, the creation of an efficient, fair, evenhanded and uniform system for determining "who serves when not all serve" and second, somewhat of a reformulation of the first, the preservation of what the Court phrased "the integrity of democratic decisionmaking against claims of individual non-compliance."

It was not unreasonable to suppose, Justice Marshall said, that both Congressional objectives might be frustrated by the virtually limitless varieties of belief subsumable under the rubric, "objection to a particular war," and that both might be jeopardized in any system of selective service which attempted to separate sincere conscientious objectors to "unjust" wars from others with spurious claims. Inherent in any such burdened system of selective conscription was the danger that military morale might be repressed and civilian cynicism aroused should "it be thought that those who go to war are chosen unfairly and capriciously." That danger was properly cognizable by Congress and its aversion a proper legislative objective. It was, therefore, "supportable for Congress to have decided that the objector to all war—to all killing in war—has a claim that is distinct enough and intense enough to justify special status while the objector to a particular war does not."

If the impermissible religious preference must appear on the face of the challenged statute, as Marshall seemed to say, or if the absence of any secular purpose must be plainly shown, which he did say, then Epperson v. Arkansas is a perplexing presentation of secular purpose analysis.

Arkansas' "anti-evolution" statute, an initiated act adopted in 1929, made it unlawful for a teacher in any state-supported school or university "to teach the theory or doctrine that mankind ascended or descended from a lower order of animals," or "to adopt or use in any such institution a textbook that teaches" that theory. The statute, said Mr. Justice Fortas, writing for a majority of the Court, was a product of "the upsurge of 'fundamentalist' religious fervor of the twenties," an adaptation of the famous *Tennessee* "monkey law" which that state had enacted in 1925 and which had been sustained by the Tennessee Supreme Court in the celebrated Scopes case of 1927.

The Arkansas statute, however, made no mention of God, the Bible, church, religion or religious beliefs. But Justice Fortas noted that a religious purpose was specifically stated on the face of the "antecedent" *Tennessee* statute and, with reverse reasoning, he extracted a sectarian purpose from the *absence* of any religious recitals in the Arkansas law. The *Tennessee* "monkey law" had candidly stated its purpose: to make it unlawful "to teach any theory that denies the story of the Divine Creation of man as taught in the Bible." "Perhaps," Justice Fortas said, the sensational publicity attendant upon the Scopes trial induced Arkansas to adopt "less explicit language." The "less explicit language" in the Arkansas statute was its total silence on the subject of religion.

Mr. Justice Fortas' "perhaps" is certainly something short of deference to a state statute, but it is not as speculative as it sounds. The Court was apparently frustrated by what Justice Black called "the pallid, unenthusiastic, even apologetic defense of the Act presented by the State in this Court." 393 U.S. at 109. (Black, J., concurring). Justice Fortas, if speculation be in order, might also have been frustrated by the fact that there was no Arkansas legislative history to which he could turn. The Arkansas statute was an initiated act proposed and approved by popular vote. It was appropriate, therefore, to consider popular responses to the teaching of Darwinism in Arkansas in 1928. Justice Fortas, however, gave us but a glimpse of the prevailing sentiment and it was not particularly persuasive. It was contained in a footnote to the Court's conclusion, "it is clear that fundamentalist sectarian conviction was and is the law's reason for existence." 393 U.S. at 107–108, n.16.

The footnote produced excerpts from an advertisement, "typical of the public appeal which was used in the campaign to secure adoption of the statute," which appeared in The Arkansas Gazette, a Little Rock newspaper, in November, 1928, and four excerpts from letters from the public published in the Gazette about the same time. The advertisement was pro-Bible and anti-atheist in its caption and in its entire content. The letters radiated the intensely evangelical fervor of their authors. There was nothing, however, to indicate that they were representative of any more than that curious but articulate class of individuals who make a profession of writing letters to the editor.

The Gazette itself apparently took an editorial stance in opposition to the initiated act, presumably for non-religious reasons. Most assuredly, there were others with strong, but non-Biblical, convictions that we are not the progeny of simian ancestors. And there are always those, with little or no faith in the Book of Genesis, who are simply amused. Surely no one would suppose that W. S. Gilbert was moved by religious emotions when he wrote, "the Darwinian man, though well behaved /At best is only a monkey shaved." The fact is that Charles Darwin's theory of man's ascent is a provocative theory. Mr. Justice Black recognized that fact in his concurring opinion. He observed that "the Darwinian theory has not merely been criticized by religionists but by scientists, and perhaps no scientist would be willing to take an oath and swear that everything announced in the Darwinian theory is unquestionably true."

Justice Black's concurrence carried considerably more persuasion. The Arkansas Supreme Court had expressed no opinion on the question whether the statute prohibited any explanation of the theory of evolution or merely prohibited teaching that the theory is true. Under the statute, left in its ambiguity, a teacher could not know, and would be put at his personal peril to determine, that which he was forbidden to teach. The statute had the vice of vagueness and Mr. Justice Black would have invalidated it for that Due Process reason alone, without reaching the "far more troublesome" First Amendment issues. He refused to accept the Court's "purpose" analysis. In his view the Court had simply chosen to close its eyes to a very perceptible secular purpose, a desire on the part of the people or the state "to withdraw from its curriculum any subject deemed too emotional and controversial for its public schools."

Justice Black also cautioned against the Court's assumption of the role of a super school board. "However wise this Court may be or may become hereafter," he said, "it is doubtful that, sitting in Washington, it can supervise and censor the curriculum of every public school in every hamlet and city in the United States. I doubt that our wisdom is so nearly infallible." Strangely enough, this is the charge which Professor Corwin had levelled at Mr. Justice Black himself. § 2.02(d), supra.

Professor Corwin's criticism was triggered by Justice Black's opinion in the *McCollum* case. Accepting the Corwin view, the same criticism could be extended to Justice Black's opinion in Engel v. Vitale and Justice Clark's opinion in Abington School Dist. v. Schempp. All were concerned with public school practices, the recital of prayers, the reading of Biblical verses or the non-curricular instruction in religion. But none were concerned with the curriculum itself. *Epperson* is quite a different case for that reason and for the more important reason that the recital of the Regents' Prayer and the Lord's Prayer and the reading of Biblical verses were religious exercises, and *McCollum*'s instruction in religion was wholly religious. In none of those cases was a secular purpose discernible. In *Epperson* a non-religious purpose was perceptible but the Court, as though it were the conscience of Arkansas, chose not to recognize it.

Epperson stands in contrast with Walz v. Tax Comm'n and with all the parochial school cases. *Walz* found a non-religious motivation with consummate ease. The New York legislature had not singled out churches as such for its real property tax exemption. Rather, it had included churches in a class of non-profit institutions, sectarian and non-sectarian—hospitals, libraries, playgrounds, professional and scientific groups and the like—engaged in eleemosynary or quasi-public pursuits.

Those quasi-public pursuits, stated somewhat abstractly as having a stabilizing influence on community life, were accepted as an adequate manifestation of a secular legislative purpose.

Unlike *Epperson*'s initiated act, the statutes before the Court in all the parochial school cases invariably recited a secular sounding purpose and the stated purpose was invariably accepted without dissent. In Board of Educ. v. Allen, e. g., it was the furtherance of educational opportunities available to the young; in Lemon v. Kurtzman, the enhancement of secular education in all schools in the state; in Committee for Public Educ. v. Nyquist and its companion 1973 cases, the preserving of a healthy and safe educational environment for all school children and the promotion of pluralism among the states' public and nonpublic schools; and, with minor variations, the same substantive purposes were restated in Meek v. Pittenger and Wolman v. Walter.

Tilton v. Richardson, the first of the three church-related college cases found a palpable secular purpose in Congress' predicated interest in the security and welfare of the United States which "require that this and future generations of American youth be assured ample opportunity for the fullest development of their intellectual capacities." The state statute in Hunt v. McNair was a verbatim replay, but in terms of the state's interest in the increase of its commerce, welfare and prosper-

[135]

ity, of the secular purpose recited in *Tilton*. And the state's purpose of supporting private higher education generally, as an economic alternative to a wholly public system, went unchallenged in Roemer v. Maryland Public Works Bd.

This quiet unanimity which descended upon the Court respecting the secular purpose of governmental aid to church-related schools did not, however, survive through the Court's struggles with the second test of Establishment, the requirement that there be a secular effect.

§ 2.04 The Secular Primary Effect and the Entanglement Alternative

The second test of Establishment speaks of a "primary" effect. That adjective, "primary", is susceptible of many meanings. Webster's abridged dictionary gives nine. The Court, in its first formulation of the primary effect test, seemed to settle for one. But in its subsequent applications of the effect test the adjective acquired a variety of meanings, some of which would astonish Mr. Webster. Though the Court has consistently repeated the test precisely as it was first articulated in Abington School Dist. v. Schempp, it has never affirmatively defined the adjective. It chose, instead, to write in converse terms of that which is non-primary in effect. From that process, the antonym emerged cloaked in other adjectives, i. e., remote, indirect, independent, incidental.

While any classification of the secular effect cases might be somewhat venturesome, we can note, but only with very modest assurance, three classes of cases, in each of which class the Court can be said to have applied the primary effect test in a definitively different sense. First are those cases in which the statute or state practice was "tainted" by a facial reference to God or by any apparent sectarian or religious purpose. Second are those in which the statute or practice was religously neutral or non-sectarian on its face. In the third class, sitting in solitary confinement, are the post-Lemon parochial school cases.

(a) The Public School Cases

Schempp itself, along with its public school predecessors, Engel v. Vitale and McCollum v. Board of Educ., is plainly within the first category. The statutes in *Schempp* required the reading of selected verses from the Holy Bible and/or the recitation of the Lord's Prayer. In *Engel* it was the recital of a state composed prayer in which a belief in God was professed and dependence upon the Almighty was acknowledged. *McCollum*'s public school classrooms were used during school hours for religious instruction by religious ministers of the various faiths. On its face each statute or program was written in terms of prayer, or respect for God, or the teaching of religious doctrines.

Schempp professed to apply the two tier test of Establishment but Mr. Justice Clark wrote for the most part of the statutes' non-secular purpose. It is difficult to determine where his purpose analysis ended and the effect began. One short segment of his opinion lent itself, however, to a secular effect rationale. Paradoxically, it came in answer to the states' contention that the statutes embodied a secular legislative purpose. Both states had asserted that the "promotion of moral values" was one of several secular reasons for the statutes' existence. It would not have been unreasonable to accept the state's secular interest in the ethical mores of its youth as a legislative motivation and it is quite reasonable to accept the inculcation of moral values as one effect of prayer programs. There may be others, non-religious in nature, as Mr. Justice Brennan observed in his concurring opinion, e. g., the fostering of harmony and tolerance among pupils, enhancing the authority of the teacher and inspiring better discipline. Indeed, it is not unreasonable to suggest that the implantation of profound moral values in students will make them better citizens, a desirable secular end. All of this can be said as well of the Regents' Prayer invalidated in *Engel* and of the religious instruction which Vashti McCollum successfully challenged.

The Biblical readings in *Schempp*, however, were not lessons in history nor were they literary exercises. They were, first and foremost, admittedly religious exercises. As such, the programs evidently failed the secular purpose test. But Justice Clark's response to the state's "moral values" argument had a primary effect twist. Even if the purpose of the exercise "is not strictly religious," he said, "it is sought to be accomplished through readings * * * from the Bible" and "the place of the Bible as an instrument of religion cannot be gainsaid." Justice Clark was simply too succinct in this significant dictum. He left too much to be inferred. But, he did condemn the use of Biblical readings, religious means, to accomplish an asserted secular end. Without professing to define the word "primary", he did apply it in its first meaning, its Latin lineage meaning of that which is first in order of development. In this sense, in the prayer and religious instruction cases, *Schempp*, *Engel* and *Mc-Collum*, the spiritual goal was necessarily first in order of development and any asserted secular effect of producing moral men and women and a better class of citizens was derivative only. It came into being after, and only if, the nonsecular objective was first achieved.

(b) Church Tax Exemptions and Sunday Closing Laws

This "primary-derivative" dichotomy, if such it were that Justice Clark suggested, was ignored in subsequent Establishment Clause cases. In Walz v. Tax Comm'n, a case which belongs in the second category, Chief Justice Burger discarded dictionary definitions and their Roman-rooted meanings. After accepting the secular purpose of the tax exemption as it appeared on the face of the statute, he gave the effect test a reverse turn. He found a primary secular effect in the avoidance of the inevitable and excessive governmental entanglement with religion which the taxing of churches would entail. "Granting tax exemptions to churches", he said "gives rise to some, but yet a lesser, involvement than taxing them." A "direct" money subsidy would create "a relationship pregnant with involvement and * * * could encompass sustained and detailed administrative relationships for enforcement of statutory standards" but the exemption creates "only minimal and remote involvement between church and state."

Thus, the tax exemption had the primary effect of reducing the evil of entanglement to an acceptable level. Obviously, however, churches derive a distinct economic advantage from a tax exemption. Exemption has the inexpungable effect of a reverse subsidy. That much was acknowledged by the Court, but exemption, Chief Justice Burger wrote, simply spares "the exercise of religion from the burden of property taxation levied on private profit institutions" and the resulting economic benefit is simply "indirect." Police and fire protection are received by houses of worship, he added, but these municipal benefits accorded churches "are no more than incidental benefits accorded all persons or institutions within a State's boundaries, along with many, many other exempt organizations."

Walz offered us "indirect" and "incidental" for that which is not primary in its non-secular effect, and in the context of minimizing entanglement the Chief Justice wrote of that which was "minimal" and "remote." The antonyms were not inapposite nor were they novel. Similar adjectives were applied in McGowan v. Maryland and its companion Blue Law cases decided in 1961, nine years before *Walz* and two years before *Schempp*. Though *Schempp* was the first case to put the Court's imprimatur on the secular purpose—secular effect analysis, *McGowan* had written explicitly of both requirements.

McGowan, like *Walz*, belongs in the second category of cases, those in which the state statute was religiously neutral and non-sectarian on its face. Maryland's Sunday closing law did contain two or three allusions to religion but, taken in their entirety, the statutes disclosed an acceptable secular purpose, that of establishing a uniform day of rest and recreation. It was a lawful public welfare or public health objective and the objective was effectively achieved. But, the selection of Sunday as the one day for cessation of labors had also the effect of advantaging the religion of those who were of the predominant Sunday-observing sects and of disadvantaging Sabbatarians and those whose religious day is other than Sunday. Church attendance by Sunday worshippers was accommodated while sincere Sabbatarians were economically burdened. They were compelled, perforce of the statute, to desist from Sunday labor and compelled, perforce of their religious faith, to close shop on the seventh day. *McGowan* addressed the Christian advantage and *McGowan*'s Free Exercise companion, Braunfeld v. Brown, 366 U.S. 599 (1961), evaluated the burden imposed upon Sabbatarians.

McGowan's initial response had the ring of the merely "incidental", the descriptive phrasing *Walz* was later to give to police protection and fire protection services provided for churches. Chief Justice Warren wrote:

> However, it is equally true that the "Establishment" Clause does not ban federal or state regulation of conduct whose reason or effect merely happens to coincide or harmonize with the tenets of some or all religions. In many instances, the Congress or state legislatures conclude that the general welfare of society, wholly apart from any religious considerations, demands such regulation. Thus, for temporal purposes, murder is illegal. And the fact that this agrees with the dictates of the Judaeo-Christian religions while it may disagree with others does not invalidate the regulation. So too with the questions of adultery and

polygamy. * * * The same could be said of theft, fraud, etc., because those offenses were also proscribed in the Decalogue. 366 U.S. at 442.

The sound of the "incidental" was most distinct in Warren's rejection of the argument—"however relevant [it] may be"—that the state had "other means at its disposal to accomplish its secular purpose, other courses that would not even remotely or incidentally give state aid to religion." Though a statute mandating that everyone rest "one day in seven, leaving the choice of the day to the individual" might suffice, the Chief Justice said, it was not the state's purpose merely to provide a "one-day-in-seven" work stoppage. It was the state's purpose "to set one day apart from all others as a day of rest, repose, recreation and tranquility—a day which all members of the family and community have the opportunity to enjoy and spend together." From Warren's view it seemed "unrealistic for enforcement purposes and perhaps detrimental to the general welfare to require a State to choose a common day of rest other than that which most persons would select of their own accord."

Implicit in the Warren response was a "primary effect" rule, the rule that a "remote" or merely "incidental" benefit to religion is not of itself adequate reason to invalidate a state regulation of conduct or a state statute which has an otherwise legitimate secular purpose and secular effect. Braunfeld v. Brown gave us one more adjective, "indirect", and applied it to characterize the burden which Sunday laws imposed upon Sabbatarians. It, too, was reiterated in *Walz*, but it was applied there to assess the benefit which tax exemption provided for churches. After acknowledging, in *Braunfeld*, the distinct economic disadvantage to which conscientious members of the Orthodox Jewish faith were subjected, Chief Justice Warren continued,

> To strike down, without the most critical scrutiny, legislation which imposes only an indirect burden on the exercise of religion, i.e., legislation which does not make unlawful the religious practice itself, would radically restrict the operating latitude of the legislature. Statutes which tax income and limit the amount which may be deducted for religious contributions impose an indirect economic burden on the observance of the religion of the citizen whose religion requires him to donate a greater amount to his church; statutes which require the courts to be closed on Saturday and Sunday impose a similar indirect burden on the observance of the religion of the trial lawyer whose religion requires him to rest on a weekday. The list of legislation of this nature is nearly limitless. 366 U.S. at 606.

The "operating latitude of the legislature" and the restraints thereon are more appropriately considered in the chapter on the Free Exercise Clause which follows. See § 3.01(b), infra.

(c) The Church-Related Elementary and Secondary School Cases

With adjectives abounding in these varying contexts, one can understand Mr. Justice Powell's exasperation with confusing refinements and misconceptions of the "primary effect" test. In Committee for Public Educ. v. Nyquist, he wrote in a footnote:

> Appellees, focusing on the term "principal or primary effect" which this Court has utilized in expressing the second prong of the three-part test * * * have argued that the Court must decide in these cases whether the "primary" effect of New York's tuition grant program is to subsidize religion or to promote these legitimate secular objectives * * *. We do not think that such metaphysical judgments are either possible or necessary. Our cases simply do not support the notion that a law found to have a "primary" effect to promote some legitimate end under the State's police power is immune from further examination to ascertain whether it also has the direct and immediate effect of advancing religion. * * * Any remaining question about the

contours of the "effect" criterion were resolved by the Court's decision in *Tilton*, in which the plurality found that the mere possiblity that a federally financed structure might be used for religious purposes 20 years hence was constitutionally unacceptable because the grant might "*in part* have the effect of advancing religion." 413 U.S. at 783–784, n.39. (Emphasis in original).

One may also understand why Justice Powell's frustration with "metaphysical judgments" found expression in a parochial school case. *Nyquist* came after Lemon v. Kurtzman and the latter's profile of the permeated parochial school. With that portrait before it in the post-*Lemon* cases, the Court, or a majority thereof, has come very close to excising the adjective "primary" from the effect test as it is applied to church-related primary and secondary schools. Those schools are now a breed apart. But it was not ever thus. For, Everson v. Board of Educ., which was the first to fashion definitive Establishment Clause principles, was itself a parochial school case.

When a state pays "the bus fares of parochial school pupils," Justice Black wrote in *Everson*, "[i]t is undoubtedly true that children are helped to get to church schools." And he was willing to concede the possibility that some children might not be sent to church schools if the parents were left to pay their children's fares while transportation to public schools was paid for by the state. The same would be true, he said, if the state were Constitutionally forbidden to provide for the parochial school and for its pupils such governmental services as police protection, fire protection, sewage disposal, highways and sidewalks. An effect rationale was evident in Justice Black's conclusion:

> Of course, cutting off church schools from these services so *separate* and so *indisputably marked off* from the religious function, would make it far more difficult for the schools to operate. But such is obviously not the purpose of the First Amendment. * * * State power is no more to be used so as to handicap religions than it is to favor them. 330 U.S. at 17–18. (Emphasis added).

For Justice Black the secular and sectarian were not inherently inseparable. He did separate one from the other, at least in the context of nonpedagogical aid. Whatever benefit reached the religious school was independent of the state's nonreligious interest in the safety and the secular welfare of its children.

The Black reasoning was applied in Board of Educ. v. Allen to sustain a New York law requiring school books to be loaned free of charge to all students in specified grades. "Perhaps free books make it more likely that some children choose to attend a sectarian school", said Justice White, "but that was true of the state-paid bus fares in

Everson and does not alone demonstrate an unconstitutional degree of support for a religious institution." Unlike bus fares, textbooks are, however, essential to the teaching process and it was asserted by appellants that in sectarian schools that process was used to teach religion. The Court repeated what has been "long recognized," that religious schools pursue two purposes, religious instruction and secular education, and it could not say, on "the meager record" before it, either that "all teaching in a sectarian school is religious or that the processes of secular and religious training are so intertwined that secular textbooks furnished to students by the public are in fact instrumental in the teaching of religion." The Court declined to hold that "this statute results in unconstitutional involvement of the State with religious instruction."

The record before the Court in Lemon v. Kurtzman, more particularly that in *Lemon*'s conjoined case, Earley v. DiCenso, was not the "meager" one with which Justice White was presented in Board of Educ. v. Allen. As already noted, the *Lemon* record was documented and considerably detailed. See § 2.02(1), supra. From that non-meager record the Court was able to conclude that the Roman Catholic schools, at the primary and secondary level, were an integral part of the spiritual mission of the Catholic Church and that in those schools secular subjects were infused with religious indoctrination, thereby to intensify the Catholic faith of their students. *Lemon* side-stepped the effect test. It invalidated the salary supplements as posing an unavoidable and excessive entanglement of government with religion. And after *Lemon* both "effect" and "entanglement" became critical criteria in parochial school cases.

Lemon's influence was evident, and powerful, in the 1973 parochial school cases, Committee for Public Educ. v. Nyquist, Sloan v. Lemon and Levitt v. Committee for Public Educ. In contrast to *Lemon*, however, the Court in 1973 wrote relatively little of entanglement and the relatively little was addressed only to the "grave potential for entanglement in the broader sense of continuing political strife over aid to religion." The Court concentrated on the effect test. Nonetheless, the entanglement potential prompted exacting scrutiny of the financial benefits which flowed to the nonpublic schools.

Nyquist was the pivotal case. It invalidated three New York programs of financial aid for nonpublic elementary and secondary schools. The first provided direct money grants to "qualifying" nonpublic schools for "maintenance and repair" of facilities to ensure student "health, welfare and safety." Qualifying schools were those which served a high concentration of pupils from low-income families. The annual grant ranged from $30 to $40 per pupil but was not to exceed 50% of the average per pupil cost of equivalent services in the public schools. The second program provided tuition reimbursements for low-income parents of children attending nonpublic schools. "Low income" was really an euphemism for poverty level income. Only those parents whose annual taxable income was less than $5,000 were eligible for the reimbursement. The amount of reimbursement was $50 per grade school child and $100 per secondary school student so long as those amounts did not exceed 50% of the actual tuition paid by the parents. The third program offered income tax relief for moderate income parents, i. e., those whose adjusted gross income was less than $25,000 per year.

Mr. Justice Powell wrote the Court's opinion. Only Justice White dissented as to the invalidation of the maintenance and repair grants. Chief Justice Burger and Justice Rehnquist joined with him in dissenting as to the invalidation of the tuition reimbursement and the tax relief provisions.

At the outset of his opinion, Justice Powell stated that the District Court had adopted a profile of the sectarian school "similar to one suggested in plaintiffs' complaint." The profile was a facsimile of *Lemon*'s portrait of the permeated parochial school. And, as if to emphasize that fact, he noted that "virtually all" of the recipients of the maintenance and repair grants were "Roman Catholic Schools in low income areas." But he acknowledged it to be "well established * * * that not every law that confers an 'indirect,' 'remote,' or 'incidental' benefit upon religious institutions is, for that reason alone, constitutionally invalid."

"Indirect," "incidental" and "remote" were *McGowan*'s and *Braunfeld*'s adjectives. But now, for the sectarian school, those words took on a different meaning. *Nyquist* repeated the *Lemon* dictate that the state must "insure" that no "part" of its grant is used to subsidize the sectarian mission of the parochial school. It was required to insure against the "possibility" of aid to the religious function. The state had made no attempt, Justice Powell stated, to restrict the maintenance and repair payments to the upkeep of facilities used for exclusively secular purposes. Then, with a devastating blow for the parochial school, he added, "nor do we think it possible within the context of these religion-oriented institutions to impose such restrictions."

"Nothing in the statute," Powell said, "* * * bars a qualifying school from paying out of state funds the salaries of employees who maintain the school chapel, or the cost of renovating classrooms in which religion is taught, or the cost of heating or lighting those same facilities." Absent appropriate restrictions, which two sentences earlier he had thought impossible to impose, Justice Powell concluded that "it simply cannot be denied that [the maintenance and repair provision] has a primary effect that advances religion in that it subsidizes directly the religious activities of the sectarian elementary and secondary schools." The Justice added a brief postscript which forecast even darker days ahead for the hapless and allegedly impoverished parochial schools. Recalling *Everson* and Board of Educ. v. Allen, he observed that some forms of aid may be channeled to the secular without providing direct aid to the religious function of the sectarian school, but he served notice that "the channel is a narrow one."

New York's tuition reimbursement and the tax relief provisions, which in the Court's view were essentially the same in purpose and effect, also foundered in those narrow straits. But, in both programs the state had sought to insure the secular effect by channelling the tuition and tax benefits directly to the parents rather than the schools. *Everson* and *Allen* were rather persuasive precedents in support of just such a device. Justice Powell found the precedents unpersuasive, however, and, in fact, irrelevant.

Everson's fare program was "so separate and so indisputably marked off from the religious function" that it reflected "a neutral posture toward religious institutions" and *Allen* "was founded upon a similar principle." Upon the record in *Allen* "there was no indication that the textbooks would be provided for anything other than purely

[152]

secular courses" and there was no reason to assume that the school authorities were unable to distinguish between secular books and religious books. In *Nyquist,* by contrast, the tuition assistance was unrestricted and no endeavor had been made to separate the secular from the sectarian educational functions or to insure that the financial aid supported only the secular. Indeed, Justice Powell insisted, "it is precisely the function of New York's law to provide assistance to private schools, the great majority of which are sectarian."

The *Everson* distinction had some substance. Bus rides to and from school have a child-safety status independent of the educational enterprise. The *Allen* distinction had a gossamer frailty. For, if the entire educational enterprise of the parochial schools were replete with religion and if their secular and sectarian functions were inextricably intertwined, as *Lemon* had discovered and *Nyquist* itself confirmed, it is difficult to understand why *Allen*'s textbooks, which aided the educational enterprise, were not of aid to the religious function —except for the sole distinguishing factor, which Powell purported to reject, that the textbooks were offered to parents and children, not to schools. After *Nyquist* the *Allen* decision called for a more explicit explanation or a more forthright justification.

There were other perplexities in the Powell distinctions. In the first part of his opinion he had conceded the legitimacy of the legislature's stated secular purpose. But now, in addressing the effect of the tuition reimbursement program, he summoned legislative "purpose" to the aid of his "effect" analysis. The admixture of purpose and effect was implicit in his conclusory assertion that it was "precisely the function" of the New York law to provide assistance to sectarian schools. It was evident in the passage which followed in the text of his opinion:

> By reimbursing parents for a portion of their tuition bill, the State seeks to relieve their financial burdens sufficiently to assure that they continue to have the option to send their children to religion-oriented schools. And while the other purposes for that aid—to perpetuate a pluralistic educational environment and to protect the fiscal integrity of over-burdened public schools—are certainly unexceptionable, the effect of the aid is unmistakably to provide desired financial support for nonpublic, sectarian institutions. 413 U.S. at 783.

Justice Powell's conclusion was certainly "unmistakable" but it was no more than a conclusion, premised upon distinctions which were inconclusive. The "financial burdens" of which New York parents were relieved were no different in nature, though perhaps in amount, than the transportation costs of which New Jersey parents were relieved in *Everson* or the textbook costs of which other New York parents, and indirectly the parochial schools themselves, were relieved in Allen v. Board of Educ. The literal import of the "primary effect" test, the test which Justice Powell approved earlier in his opinion, became considerably obscured. It would have certainly clarified matters, and surely it would not have been injudicious, had Justice Powell simply stated without equivocation that on this issue of tuition reimbursement the "primary" part of the primary effect test was inappropriate.

That would appear to be the realistic effect of his holding. Perhaps it is precisely what he intended. For, he wrote in the quoted paragraph of the "effect," not the "primary" effect of New York's tuition program. Mr. Justice White took him at his word. Justice White reminded the majority that the test, theretofore fashioned by the Court, was "one of 'primary' effect, not *any* effect", and he declared that the *Nyquist* Court had made "no attempt at that ultimate judgment."

Justice Powell's response was his footnote, n. 39, set forth above, the footnote in which he stated that a statute, which has been found to have a "primary" effect of promoting some legitimate end "under the state's police power," does not thereby acquire immunity "from further examination" to ascertain whether it also has the "direct" and "immediate" effect of advancing religion. The statement was undoubtedly true but it presented nothing new. *Walz* had recognized that principle and *Walz* concluded that the economic advantage which religious institutions derived from tax exemptions was indirect and incidental in effect.

Walz, however, engaged in "further examination." It reviewed the history of church tax exemptions and it analyzed the effect which exemptions produced in avoiding or diminishing entanglements between church and state. In dealing with the tuition provisions, the *Nyquist* Court, by contrast, seemed satisfied with the rather complacent assertion that the "effect" of the aid was "to provide financial support for nonpublic, sectarian institutions." A try at distinguishing *Walz* was reserved for the Court's invalidation of the third part of the New York statutes, the tax relief package. But, if *Walz* were a really relevant precedent, it was as pertinent to the tuition program as it was to the tax relief provisions.

The Powell footnote was, by its terms, intended to clarify the Court's "effect" test and, presumably, to add some measure of support for the categorical conclusion which sprang, almost impromptu, from the Court's application of that test. It was a cryptic footnote. It enveloped the primary effect test in a semantical cloud. In the rather ambivalent "police power" sentence Justice Powell seemed to suggest, but did not state expressly, that the tuition reimbursement program had a "direct" and "immediate" effect of advancing religion. If he really meant that which he seemed to imply, the difficulties inherent in his various distinctions were truly compounded.

For one, as vexing as it might be to understand why a very modest amount of tuition assistance offered to parents of terribly low income was less indirect in its aid to private schools than textbooks made available to children, the more vexing it is to comprehend why tuition assistance for parents constituted direct funding of religion while church tax exemptions did not constitute direct funding of churches and, therefore, religion per se. Churches are, after all, purely religious entities.

For another, Justice Powell declared that "metaphysical judgments" as to the "primary" effect of the tuition program were neither "possible" or "necessary." Two sentences later he asserted that Sunday Closing Laws were upheld in McGowan v. Maryland "not because their effect was, first, to promote the legitimate interest in a universal day of rest and recreation and only secondarily to assist religious interests; instead, approval flowed from the finding * * * that [such laws] had only a remote and incidental effect advantageous to religious institutions." One must really wonder why ascertainment of the "primary" effect of New York's tuition program involved "metaphysical judgments" while ascertainment of the "direct" and "indirect" effect of church tax exemptions or the "remote" and "incidental" effect of Sunday laws required only non-metaphysical judgments. And it is not at all unreasonable to suggest that "indirect," "remote" and "incidental" were, in the pre-*Nyquist* cases, plainly nothing more than Court-created synonyms for that which is non-primary in its effect. But, however "metaphysical" or non-metaphysical these judgments may be, in the end there is one unmistakable fact which cannot be ignored. *Nyquist* was a parochial school case. *Walz* and *McGowan* were not parochial school cases.

Of the four opinions written in *Nyquist* on the tuition reimbursement issue, that of Mr. Justice White was first in frankness and first in objectivity. Too many of the majority's distinctions were distinctions without a substantial difference. Justice White's conclusion that the Court had transformed the "primary" effect test into an "any" effect test was faithfully frank and it was compelling. All that was written in *Nyquist*, however, was written in the context of state programs which were challenged as providing financial aid to elementary and secondary sectarian schools. Adjectives and their antonyms, such as primary and secondary, direct and indirect, immediate and remote or incidental, may be suitable to ascertain the effect of church tax exemptions, of Sunday Closing Laws, or of Bible reading and prayers in public schools, but in *Nyquist* Justice Powell's "effect" doctrine effectively rendered those adjectives and antonyms superfluous when dealing with cash payments, by government to parents, which have the potential of providing financial aid for sectarian schools.

The stringent discipline of *Nyquist's* parochial school lesson was manifested in Justice Powell's reaction to three "subsidiary arguments" which he chose to address "in view of the novelty of the question." The three arguments were not so novel and they were hardly subsidiary. Justice Powell responded in rather summary fashion.

The first was really a relative of appellees' principal argument that the tuition assistance was for parents, not for schools, and its validity was, therefore, certified by *Everson* and *Allen*. But here the argument was re-presented with emphasis on the fact that it was a true "reimbursement," not a direct contribution merely routed "in advance" through the parents to the schools. It was of no consequence, Justice Powell wrote, that reimbursement was provided only "after" tuition had already been paid—so that "the parent is not a mere conduit * * * but is absolutely free to spend the money he receives in any manner he wishes." For he said:

> [I]f the grants are offered as an incentive to parents to send their children to sectarian schools by making unrestricted cash payments to them, the Establishment Clause is violated

whether or not the actual dollars given eventually find their way into the sectarian institutions. Whether the grant is labeled a reimbursement, a reward, or a subsidy, its substantive impact is still the same. In sum, we agree with the conclusion of the District Court that "[w]hether he gets it during the current year, or as reimbursement for the past year, is of no constitutional importance." 413 U.S. at 786–787.

Brevity is admirable but clarity essential. In his brief paragraph Justice Powell left principles unclear. Of course, *Everson* and *Allen* provided the same "incentive to parents to send their children to sectarian schools." Was Justice Powell now suggesting, however, that *Everson* did not offer "unrestricted" cash payments and that *Allen* did not offer "cash" payments? The distinction may be acceptable as to *Everson* but one would still be left to wonder why minimal cash payments to low income parents is Constitutionally offensive while the monetary equivalent in the form of textbooks for all parents, regardless of income, is permissible.

The second subsidiary argument was a computerized one which offered inbuilt statistical guarantees that the tuition reimbursement could not possibly be of actual financial aid to the religious function of the church-related schools. Since the New York statute limited reimbursement to 50% of any parent's tuition payments and since only 30% of the total cost of nonpublic education' was derived from tuition, with the remainder coming from contributions, endowments and similar gifts, the maximum tuition reimbursement was only 15% of the educational costs in the nonpublic schools. And, since the state's compulsory education laws by necessity required significantly more than 15% of school time to be devoted to teaching secular courses, appellees argued, the statute itself provided "a statistical guarantee of neutrality."

A variant of the same argument had been offered respecting the "maintenance and repair grants." It was there rejected both factually and in principle—factually because by their statutory measure the grants could conceivably have exceeded the actual costs of the maintenance and repair of secular facilities. Here Justice Powell rejected the argument in principle, curtly noting that "[o]ur cases * * * have long since foreclosed the notion that mere statistical assurances will suffice to sail between the Scylla and Charybdis of 'effect' and 'entanglement.'" However curt his observation, the principle had a significant semblance of support in *Lemon*'s companion case, Earley v. DiCenso. See 403 U.S. at 619.

In the third subsidiary argument appellees underscored the socially appealing fact that only parents of very low income were aided by the statute. Appellees forcefully asserted that, without state assistance, the Constitutional right of those parents to have their children educated in a religious environment would be "diminished or even denied." That Constitutional right had been established in Pierce v. Society of the Sisters, 268 U.S. 510 (1925), and it was turned in Wisconsin v. Yoder, 406 U.S. 205 (1972), into a fundamental parental and Free Exercise guarantee. Justice Powell acknowledged the inherent tension which exists between the First Amendment's religion clauses but he simply refused to release the tensity on the Establishment side. He replied, without further ado, that the state could not "enhance the opportunities of the poor to choose between public and nonpublic education" by taking a step "which can only be regarded as one 'advancing' religion."

Chief Justice Burger evidently considered it a small step for the state and an equitable step for the parents of nonpublic school children. State aid to individuals, he stated, "stands on an entirely different footing from direct aid to religious institutions." The tuition and tax provisions were no more than legitimate general welfare programs under which benefits were made available to individuals and, under *Everson* and *Allen*, they remained Constitutional "even though many of those individuals may elect to use those benefits in ways that 'aid' religious instruction or worship."

Nor was it possible to extract a "constitutionally meaningful" distinction from the fact that

Everson's bus rides and *Allen*'s textbooks were made available to all children, while New York's tax and tuition benefits were available only to parents of nonpublic school children. The Court's endeavor to do so simply exalted "form over substance." It was beyond dispute, he said, that the parents of public school students received the "benefit" of having their children educated entirely at state expense and the New York statutes simply sought to equalize the "benefit." The Chief Justice concluded that it was "no more than simple equity to grant relief to parents who support the public schools they do not use."

Chief Justice Burger perceived no discernible difference between the tuition reimbursement plan and the tax relief provisions. He found both compatible with the Establishment Clause. For purposes of determining whether the statutes had "the effect of advancing religion", Justice Powell agreed that in practical terms there was little difference between the two programs. Having invalidated the tuition statute, he might have rested his case against the tax relief provisions with that brief observation. But, in support of the tax program, appellees had fixed their point of focus on Walz v. Tax Comm'n. And *Walz* had sustained tax relief for churches and temples—complete relief. So, Justice Powell undertook to distinguish *Walz*.

He sought a distinction in the long history of church tax exemptions, which Chief Justice Burger had surveyed in *Walz*, a history which had revealed an universal approval of exemptions for church property both before and after the adoption of the First Amendment. But, Justice Powell "knew" of no historical precedents for New York's "recently promulgated" tax relief program. He conceded, however, as had *Walz* before him, that "historical acceptance without more would not alone have sufficed" to sustain church tax exemptions. What, then, was there in novelty or recency which might dictate defeat of the tax relief statute? Once more Powell pursued the anomalous process of stressing the "purpose" of the New York program to formulate his "effect" test.

In an historical context, if taxation of churches "was regarded" as a form of hostility toward religion, then exemption was the wiser course to achieve religious neutrality. Exemption of church property from taxation conferred a benefit, "albeit an indirect and incidental one", Justice Powell wrote, but that aid was "a product not of any purpose to support or to subsidize, but of a fiscal relationship designed to minimize involvement and entanglement between Church and State."

Justice Powell's distillation of the principles of Walz v. Tax Comm'n was precise and accurate. But, the distinction suggested was disconcerting. The tax relief program, which concededly was never "regarded" by the New York legislature as a form of favoritism for religion, was also designed to avoid confrontations between church and state. Like the tuition reimbursement plan, it neither created nor required any relationship between the state and any church or any church school. Nonetheless, Justice Powell insisted, without amplification, that the aid inherent in the tax relief program was the product of a "purpose" to support and subsidize sectarian schools. And he added that the granting of tax benefits under the New York statute "would tend to increase rather than limit the involvement between Church and State."

Both packages were wrapped in his conclusion that "neither form of aid [tuition reimbursement or tax relief] is sufficiently restricted to assure that it will not have the impermissible effect of advancing the sectarian activities of religious schools."

Unlike the majority's commingling of purpose with effect, Justice Rehnquist's dissent presented a pure effect analysis. In terms of effect he found the Court's invalidation of the New York tax relief program completely at odds with Walz v. Tax Comm'n. Justice Rehnquist wrote:

> Here the effect of the tax benefit is trebly attenuated as compared with the outright exemption considered in *Walz*. There the result was a complete forgiveness of taxes, while here the result is merely a reduction in taxes.

There the ultimate benefit was available to an actual house of worship, while here even the ultimate benefit redounds only to a religiously sponsored school. There the churches themselves received the direct reduction in the tax bill, while here it is only the parents of the children who are sent to religiously sponsored schools who receive the direct benefit. 413 U.S. at 807. (Rehnquist, J., dissenting in part).

Churches and synagogues are surely religious, and solely religious. So Walz v. Tax Comm'n was willing to assume. For, Chief Justice Burger declined to rest his *Walz* decision on "the social welfare services" performed by churches. Elementary and secondary sectarian schools serve a dual purpose, secular education and religious instruction. That fact was stated in *Allen* and recognized in *Everson*. It poses a paradox to sustain financial aid, "albeit indirect and incidental", for the wholly religious churches and synagogues and invalidate aid, even that which is apparently indirect, for the dual-purposed parochial schools. It has been evident ever since *Everson* that direct governmental funding of parochial schools is Constitutionally impermissible. The significance of *Nyquist* is that it pronounced, in its own indirect way but in realistic result, a second precept: the state is forbidden to "seek", Justice Powell's verb, to accomplish, in the form of tuition reimbursements and tax relief for parents, that which it is forbidden to do directly in the form of funding.

Whether we find complete persuasion in the Rehnquist effect analysis or adequate sufficiency in the Powell distinctions, do we not come back again to the simple notation that *Nyquist* was a parochial school case and *Walz* was not? *Nyquist* was a consequence of *Lemon*'s finding that the entire elementary and secondary sectarian school system was permeated with religion. *Lemon* preached entanglement principles in the context of state subsidies and supplements for sectarian school teachers and, under the guise of a "purchase of secular services", for the sectarian schools themselves.

In that context the entanglement doctrine had a rational appeal. The Pennsylvania and Rhode Island statutes created a relationship, replete with potential confrontations, between state and sectarian schools or sectarian school teachers. The permeated character of the parochial schools dictated the need for surveillance. But, in *Nyquist*, as noted, no such relationship was created by New York's tuition or tax programs. The possibility of confrontations between church and state did not exist. Appropriately, therefore, *Nyquist* turned to the "effect" of the New York programs.

To ascertain "effect" *Nyquist* first sorted out a legislative "purpose" of providing financial aid for the financially pressed parochial schools, and from

Lemon it extracted that part of the latter's holding which dictated that the state "must insure" that subsidies offered to teachers do not promote the religious function of the church-related schools. Whether or not *Nyquist* took from *Lemon*'s lesson an "any" effect test, the test it did apply was one which instinctively foreordained the non-secular "effect" of any form of state monetary assistance which is not sufficiently restricted to assure that it does not advance the religious activities of sectarian schools.

Tuition reimbursements and tax relief for parents, however "indirect" we may believe them to be, do not, according to *Nyquist*, per se provide that assurance. Cold statistics and clear statutory limitations, which concededly confined tuition reimbursement and tax relief to an amount far less than the cost of the secular education provided by the parochial schools, will not suffice. And, unlike the loan of secular educational materials to students or parents, materials which could be used only in the schools, the tuition reimbursements were post-payment grants which the parent could spend as he or she saw fit. It is well-nigh impossible to conceive of any restrictions upon tuition reimbursement and tax relief, short of the absolute exclusion of parents of parochial school students, which might satisfy the assurance which the Court demanded.

The infirmities which, in the majority's view, infested New York's tuition reimbursement program proved fatal for a similar scheme which had been enacted in Pennsylvania subsequent to the Court's decision in Lemon v. Kurtzman. In a relatively brief opinion in Sloan v. Lemon, Justice Powell found "no constitutionally significant distinctions" between the New York and Pennsylvania programs. The Pennsylvania tuition reimbursement law was invalidated on the authority of *Nyquist*.

Levitt v. Committee for Public Educ. was the last of the 1973 trilogy of nonpublic elementary and secondary school cases. It presented yet another New York program of financial assistance for nonpublic schools, a program which provided reimbursement—fixed at a "per-pupil" rate of $27 for the lower grades and $45 for grades seven through twelve—for specified testing and recordkeeping which had been "mandated" by state law. Chief Justice Burger wrote the Court's opinion. It provoked only one dissent, that of Mr. Justice White, the Court's consistent advocate of equality for all children, regardless of creed or race.

The "mandated services", for which the state sought to reimburse the private schools, included not only the administration, grading and reporting of two types of scholastic tests but also the maintenance of records and submission of reports respecting school personnel qualifications, student enrollment and student health. But, of these mandated services "by far the most expensive" for the nonpublic schools was the administration, grading, compiling and reporting of the results of tests and examinations. The latter were of two kinds, the one, state prepared examinations, e.g., "Regents Examinations", and the other, traditional teacher-prepared tests which were drafted by the private school teachers for the purpose of measuring student progress in subjects required to be taught under state law. The overwhelming majority of testing in nonpublic as well as public schools was in the second category.

The Court conceded that some of the compensated services were secular in nature and some potentially religious. The various services, however, had been placed, unassorted, in a single legislative package. And, remuneration was offered in a lump sum without allocation of payment among the specific services which the state required of the nonpublic schools. Allocation of costs to services, or the reduction of the "per-pupil allotment" to an amount "corresponding to the actual costs incurred in performing reimbursable secular services", Chief Justice Burger wrote, is "a legislative, not a judicial function." And if, per *Nyquist*, "any part" of the program served to advance the religious function of the sectarian school, the entire program must fail. Appropriately, then, the Chief Justice set his sights on an already tattered target, the teaching process of the parochial schools. His aim was predictably accurate.

Chief Justice Burger began his analysis where he had begun in *Lemon* and where Mr. Justice Powell did in *Nyquist*—with the profile of the parochial school. With the profile before him, the singular issue of teacher-prepared testing admitted of brevity. And the Chief Justice was brief. He needed only *Lemon* and *Nyquist* to support his holding that the *Levitt* program suffered from the same Constitutional flaws which *Nyquist* found in the "maintenance and repair" grants.

Any program of internal testing, designed to measure student achievement, has "an obviously integral role * * * in the total teaching process", the Court held, and it could not ignore "the substantial risk that these examinations, prepared by teachers under the authority of religious institutions, will be drafted with an eye, unconsciously or otherwise, to inculcate students in the religious precepts of the sponsoring church." The state was, as in *Lemon*, constitutionally compelled to assure that the state-supported activity was not being used for religious indoctrination. Having failed to do so, Chief Justice Burger wrote, the Court was left with no choice "but to hold that [the New York statute] constitutes an impermissible aid to religion." That was so, he added, "because the aid that will be devoted to secular functions is not identifiable and separable from aid to sectarian activities."

Everson and *Allen* were again distinguished but this time with a little more persuasion than *Nyquist* had offered. Bus rides and state-provided textbooks are of a substantially different character, Burger said, since they, unlike routine teacher-prepared tests, are not an integral part of the teaching process. The Court's equation of "textbooks" and "bus rides" was rather surprising. Textbooks, unlike bus rides, are an integral and primary part of the teaching process. But the Chief Justice's further distinction between textbooks and the role of the teacher in the teaching process had a saving consistency. He repeated what he had written in *Lemon*: "In terms of potential for involving some aspect of faith or morals in secular subjects, a textbook's content is ascertainable, but a teacher's handling of a subject is not."

Finally, in two sentences the Court disposed of appellants' contention that the state should be permitted to pay for any activity "mandated" by state law. "The essential inquiry in each case," the Chief Justice said, "* * * is whether the challenged state aid has the primary purpose or effect of advancing religion or religious education or whether it leads to excessive entanglement by the State in the affairs of the religious institu-

[172]

tion." And that inquiry "would be irreversibly frustrated if the Establishment Clause were read as permitting a State to pay for whatever it requires a private school to do."

In *Levitt*, Chief Justice Burger wrote of the inescapable potential for sectarian indoctrination which inheres in examinations prepared by instructors who are subject to the authority of religious institutions. In *Lemon*, the Chief Justice had written of the great difficulty which parochial school teachers, who are subject to the discipline of religious superiors, would inevitably experience in remaining religiously neutral. In no case had the Court ever intimated any qualms about the ability of public school teachers to maintain religious neutrality in the performance of their public school duties. In Meek v. Pittenger, two years after *Levitt*, a majority of the Court parted with part of its faith in the competency of public school personnel to adhere to its professional commitment to wholly secular instruction.

The *Meek* Court was back in Pennsylvania, *Lemon*'s territory. Though we might have simply assumed that *Lemon*'s portrait of the parochial school did not have Dorian Gray's changeable characteristic, the *Lemon* profile was again placed on display. But, on this occasion the Court took a particularly dim view of the fact that more than 75% of the Pennsylvania's nonpublic schools were church-related or religiously affiliated educational institutions. It thrice emphasized that the primary beneficiaries were nonpublic schools with a predominant sectarian character. The relevancy of the Court's computation was questionable.

Of course, the numerical predominance of sectarian schools might be pertinent in ascertaining whether the legislative "purpose" was to advance the cause of religion. But, whether 5% or 75% of the class of potential beneficiaries were church affiliated should make no difference—a point which Chief Justice Burger had argued in *Nyquist*—in applying the primary "effect" test. *Meek* did not suggest, however, that a numerical count of potential religious beneficiaries was of controlling significance. But, the count itself would seem to indicate that the Court, prompted by percentages, was prepared, as was the *Nyquist* majority, to scrutinize, with most exacting care, any state program which carried the potential of advancing the religious mission of the sectarian schools. With the exception of one Pennsylvania program, *Meek* did precisely that.

Three programs of public assistance for private schools or for private school children were challenged in *Meek*. The first was the loan of secular textbooks to children in private elementary and secondary schools. The second, the loan, directly to the nonpublic schools, of "instructional materials and equipment", e. g., maps, charts, recordings, films, projectors, recorders and laboratory instruments. Third was the program of "auxiliary services", e. g., counselling, testing, psychological services, speech and hearing therapy and services for the improvement of the educationally disadvantaged, such as teaching English as a second language—all provided directly to nonpublic school children by professional public school personnel. The services were provided, however, only on the nonpublic school premises.

The three programs tripartited the Court itself in its application of the tripartite test. There was the triumvirate of Chief Justice Burger, Justice White and Justice Rehnquist, which would have sustained all three programs. There was the Douglas—Brennan—Marshall coalition which would have invalidated all three programs. And there were the middlemen, Mr. Justice Stewart, the author of the Court's opinion, Justice Blackmun and Justice Powell, who sustained the textbook program but rejected both the loan of instructional materials and equipment and the provision for auxiliary services.

The financial benefit of Pennsylvania's textbook program, like New York's in *Allen*, was to parents and children, not the nonpublic schools. Only textbooks which were acceptable for use "in any public, elementary, or secondary school of the Commonwealth" were made available to private school students. And in the record before the Court there was no suggestion that the texts would be used for anything other than purely secular purposes. In sum, the textbook loan program was in every material respect identical to the loan program approved in *Allen*. Pennsylvania, like New York, merely made available "to all children the benefits of a general program to lend school books free of charge." Justice Stewart did not pause, however, to re-evaluate *Allen* in the light of *Lemon* and of *Nyquist*. *Allen* was simply accepted with precedential respect.

Mr. Justice Stewart was not so deferential when he dealt with the loan of instructional materials and equipment to the nonpublic schools. He did acknowledge, as a principle established in the Court's cases from *Everson* to *Nyquist*, that "as part of general legislation made available to all students" a state may include church-related schools in programs providing "secular and non-ideological services", e.g., bus transportation, school lunches and public health facilities. Such services were "unrelated to the primary, religious-oriented educational function of the sectarian school" and any resulting benefit which reached the religious function of the nonpublic school was "indirect" and "incidental". By contrast, the "massive aid" which the present program provided for religious schools in Pennsylvania was "neither indirect nor incidental".

The District Court had found most of the instructional materials to be self-policing "in that starting as secular, nonideological and neutral, they will not change in use." Justice Stewart accepted the District Court's characterization. To be sure, Bunsen burners may be used to distill holy water or movie projectors for a re-run of "Our Lady of Fatima" for its religious inspiration. Justice Stewart, however, did not indulge in extravagant speculation. The parochial school system is pervasively religious. And he had already noted that just under $12 million of "direct" aid had been appropriated to support the instructional material program. Despite the self-policing, neutral character of the materials and equipment, he found it realistically impossible to separate the secular educational functions from the predominantly religious role performed by church-related schools. He found it impossible to classify those "substantial" amounts of "direct" support as aid to the secular function only. However carefully it may be earmarked for secular purposes, Stewart concluded, aid which flows "to an institution in which religion is so pervasive that a substantial portion of its functions are subsumed in the religious mission" has the impermissible effect of advancing religion.

What now of the "self-policing" textbook program? Textbooks, Justice Stewart had noted earlier in his opinion were lent to students, not to schools. The loan of instructional material and equipment was offered directly to the nonpublic school. It was the kind of distinction which Justice Powell had eschewed when evaluating New York's tuition and tax relief programs. Indeed, it was the kind of distinction Justice Powell had rejected.

Justice Stewart foresook the "effect" test in his analysis of the "auxiliary services". He turned to the third tier of Establishment, excessive government entanglement with religion. Wisely so. The auxiliary services were made available to disadvantaged children, children with educational impediments and those who were functionally deficient. It was a child welfare program with all the earmarks of *Everson*'s child safety solution. But, the services were performed on nonpublic school premises and in most instances in the permeated atmosphere of the parochial school. Justice Stewart unfurled a novel and surprisingly sensitive entanglement principle.

The District Court had written rather convincingly both in terms of effect and in terms of entanglement. It had emphasized that the "auxiliary services" were offered directly to the children and that they were expressly limited to such as were secular, neutral and nonideological. It had held that any resulting benefits to the church-related schools were "merely incidental and indirect". The program seemed secure under the effect test.

The lower court's findings and its analysis seemed to provide equal security for its non-entanglement conclusion. There were no contacts be-

tween the public school personnel and the personnel of the sectarian schools. Recognizing logistical
realities, the state had quite sensibly chosen to
provide travelling therapists rather than transport
travelling pupils. The state exercised the same
control over its professional personnel serving nonpublic school students as it exercised over public
school employees generally. The District Court
had concluded, therefore, that continuing surveillance of its travelling therapists and travelling
counsellors was not necessary either to insure that
the statute's secular limitations were observed or
to guarantee that the public school professional
had not "succumb[ed] to sectarianization of his or
her professional work."

Lemon v. Kurtzman, together with Earley v.
DiCenso, had told us that it was not sufficient for
the state to "assume" that subsidized teachers in
church-related schools would succeed in segregating
their religious beliefs and religious commitments
from their secular educational duties. The state
must be certain, the Court held, that the subsidized teachers do not inculcate religion. To do
so, a comprehensive, discriminating, and continuing surveillance would inevitably be required to
insure that the secular restrictions, spelled out in
the statute, were obeyed.

Lemon wrote of Catholic parochial school teachers. It wrote of teachers who were predominantly
of the same religious faith as their institutional

employer; teachers chosen by a parish pastor and approved by the surrogate of a Roman Catholic bishop; teachers who, if the selection guidelines of the diocese were effective, were inspired by the message of the Gospel, prepared to promote the proselytizing mission of the Catholic Church and dedicated to the rearing of children in the Catholic faith. And, most noteworthy, *Lemon* wrote of teachers who were subject to "the direction and discipline" of religious authorities.

Lemon's portrait of the parochial school teacher bore no resemblance whatever to the public school teacher or to the professional personnel of the public school. Nonetheless, with a questionable sequitur, Mr. Justice Stewart held that the inevitable need for surveillance of the subsidized parochial school teacher was required as well for the professional therapists and counsellors in the employ of the public school. Though the contacts of the public school personnel were only with children and not at all with sectarian school personnel, the need for surveillance arose simply because the public school professionals performed their professional services within the precincts of the religiously permeated parochial school. The atmosphere itself had a religiously permeating influence.

Justice Stewart stated his premise and his conclusion concisely:

The fact that the teachers and counselors providing auxiliary services are employees of the public intermediate unit, rather than of the church-related schools in which they work, does not substantially eliminate the need for continuing surveillance. To be sure, auxiliary services personnel, because not employed by the nonpublic schools, are not directly subject to the discipline of a religious authority. * * * But they are performing important educational services in schools in which education is an integral part of the dominant sectarian mission and in which an atmosphere dedicated to the advancement of religious belief is constantly maintained. * * * The potential for impermissible fostering of religion under these circumstances, although somewhat reduced, is nonetheless present. To be certain that auxiliary teachers remain religiously neutral, as the Constitution demands, the State would have to impose limitations on the activities of auxiliary personnel and then engage in some form of continuing surveillance to ensure that those restrictions were being followed. 421 U.S. at 371–372.

It must be noted that Justice Stewart wrote only of "teachers" and "counselors." The statute, however, also provided for therapists and for speech and hearing services. In a footnote Stewart stated that the provision for "speech and hearing services", at least to the extent such services are diagnostic, "seems" to fall within the class of general welfare services for children which are permissible regardless of the incidental benefit which may accrue to the sectarian school. He chose not to pass judgment on the validity of the speech and hearing services. He declined to sever those services from the counseling and remedial instruction provisions and, therefore, the fault he found in the latter was fatal for the entire auxiliary services program.

In a concluding paragraph Justice Stewart found the "political entanglement" concept also of service. The prospect of repeated confrontations, as annual appropriations were required, between proponents and opponents of the auxiliary services program provided "successive opportunities for political fragmentation and division along religious lines." Accordingly, the "potential for political entanglement, together with the administrative entanglement which would be necessary to ensure that auxiliary-services personnel remain strictly neutral and non-ideological when functioning in church-related schools compels the conclusion that [the statute] violates the constitutional prohibition against laws 'respecting an establishment of religion.' "

Lemon found the peril of entanglement in the teaching process of the subsidized parochial school teacher, teaching in the parochial school. *Meek* reached the peril point when the public school teacher entered the sectarian school. As there are those who would argue that *Nyquist*, in its invalidation of New York's tuition and tax programs, took the effect test to excess, there are those who would assert that *Meek*, in its invalidation of Pennsylvania's "auxiliary services" program, carried the entanglement test to extremes. Chief Justice Burger, the author of *Lemon*, belonged to both groups. His *Nyquist* dissent, however, was tepid as compared to his calid criticism of *Meek*'s entanglement analysis.

Chief Justice Burger found the majority's entanglement conclusion simply "extravagant." There was, he said, absolutely no support in the record, in ordinary human experience, or in history, for the Court's conclusion that the services of state-selected professionals, offering remedial assistance for "all" children contains "the same potential for administrative entanglement or divisive political confrontation" which concerned the Court in *Lemon*. Indeed, Burger saw "as much potential for divisive political debate in opposition to the crabbed attitude the Court shows in this case."

In the Chief Justice's view, the Court's holding was particularly offensive because it penalized "children" who had the misfortune "to have to cope with the learning process under extraordinarily heavy physical and psychological burdens, for the

[183]

most part congenital." And it was the more offensive because the penalty struck them "not because of any act of theirs but because of their parents' choice of religious exercise."

The "melancholy consequence" of the Court's decision, Burger concluded, was "to force the parent to choose between the 'free exercise' of a religious belief by opting for a sectarian education for his child or to forego the opportunity for his child to learn to cope with—or overcome—serious congenital learning handicaps, through remedial assistance financed by his taxes." Affluent parents can escape the conflict by employing private teaching specialists. But, all others will be forced "to make a choice between their judgment as to their children's spiritual needs and their temporal need for special remedial learning assistance." The Chief Justice remained hopeful that at some future date the Court will come "to a more enlightened and tolerant view of the First Amendment's guarantee of free exercise of religion."

All of the Court's holdings in *Nyquist* and *Meek* had the concurrence of six or more Justices. Accepting the *Lemon—Nyquist—Meek* precedents and ignoring the controversy they engendered, there was little left for Mr. Justice Blackmun to do in Wolman v. Walter—except sum up.

The *Wolman* Court was presented with an Ohio legislative package containing six parcels of aid for nonpublic elementary and secondary school students. The package was quite obviously designed to conform to the teachings of *Nyquist* and *Meek*. Each parcel was carefully wrapped in the form of aid to students rather than to schools. But, it was noted that 96% of those students were enrolled in sectarian schools, that more than 92% attended Catholic schools and that there was no significant difference between the schools involved here and those in Lemon v. Kurtzman.

Once more the Court was frightfully fragmented. The views of the Justices stretched from that of Justices White and Rehnquist, who would have sustained all the challenged components, to that of Mr. Justice Brennan who would have invalidated all. The Constitutional segments were sustained by votes ranging from 6 to 3 to 8 to 1. The unconstitutional parcels carried the condemnation of 6 to 3 and 5 to 4 majorities.

Mr. Justice Blackmun delivered the opinion of the Court in litany-like fashion and with a very acute adherence to the *Lemon—Nyquist—Meek* precedents. The recital produced a little more aid than was sanctioned in *Meek* and, in the bus service part of the program, a little less than would seem to have been sanctioned in *Everson.* The Court's holdings are summarized herein in accordance with Justice Blackmun's arrangement and with the captions he gave to each program.

Textbooks: The system for the loan of textbooks to individual students bore a striking resemblance to the programs approved in *Allen* and in *Meek*. The only arguable difference lay in the statutory definition of "textbook" as "any book or book substitute." Appellants had argued that a "book substitute" might include equipment and materials which may not constitutionally be loaned. The Court found the distinction untenable in the light of the statute's separate provision for instructional materials and equipment, and in the light of the parties' stipulation defining textbooks as "limited to books, reusable workbooks, or manuals." Stare decisis then prevailed. The Court refused to overrule *Allen* and the textbook part of Meek v. Pittenger. The Ohio book program was constitutional.

Testing and Scoring: The state has an unquestionable interest in assuring that the nonpublic schools satisfy the state's minimum educational standards. The testing and scoring program was enacted to protect that interest. It provided for the use by nonpublic school students of such standardized tests and scoring services as were in use in the public schools of the state. Nonpublic school personnel were not involved in either the drafting or the scoring of the tests. Nor did the statute authorize any payment to the nonpublic school or to nonpublic school personnel for the costs of administering the tests.

Levitt v. Committee for Public Educ. was distinguished. In *Levitt* New York's statutory scheme provided for reimbursements of church-sponsored schools for the expenses of teacher-prepared testing. And in *Levitt* no means were available to assure that "internally prepared tests" were free of religious instruction. By contrast, under the Ohio program the nonpublic school did not control the content of the test or its result. That absence of control was a sufficient safeguard against "the use of the test as a part of religious teaching." Similarly, Justice Powell added, that absence of control eliminated "the need for the supervision that gives rise to excessive entanglement." The testing and scoring provisions were constitutional.

Levitt was again distinguished in Committee for Public Educ. v. Regan, supra, a 5–4 decision, which deemphasized the emphasis Justice Blackmun had put on the fact that the Ohio program provided no reimbursement for the nonpublic school and on the fact that nonpublic school personnel were not involved in the scoring of the tests. The *Regan* Court sustained a revised, post-*Levitt* New York program which did provide reimbursement for services rendered by nonpublic schools in the administration of three types of tests, all of which addressed a secular academic subject.

The first were state prepared tests, graded by state personnel. The risk that those examinations might be used for religious purposes the Court found non-existent. Tests of the second type were graded by nonpublic school employees but they consisted entirely of objective, multiple choice questions, which could be graded by machine and, even if graded by hand, the schools were afforded no more control over the results than if the tests were graded by the state. The third group of tests, based on state courses of study, was also graded by nonpublic school personnel but consisted largely or entirely of objective questions with multiple choice answers. Some of those tests, however, occasionally contained an essay question. The Court accepted the lower court's conclusion that there was no more than a "minimal" chance that grading of answers to state-drafted questions in secular subjects could or would be used to gauge a student's grasp of religious ideas. The risk of religious use was further minimized by the fact that the completed and graded examinations were required to be submitted for off-school-premises review by the state department of education. Having determined that the grading of secular tests furnished by the state was a function that had a secular purpose and primarily a secular effect, that conclusion, the Court held, was not subject to change simply because the state paid the school for performing the grading function.

Diagnostic Services: Speech and hearing and psychological diagnostic services were provided within the nonpublic school. The diagnostic personnel were all employees of the local board of education, with the exception of physicians who were retained by the board of education on a contract basis. The purpose of the services was solely to determine the pupil's hearing, speech or psychological deficiency and his need for assistance. Treatment of any discovered defect took place outside the nonpublic school premises.

"This Court's decisions", Justice Blackmun wrote, "contain a common thread to the effect that the provision of health services to all school children —public and nonpublic—does not have the primary effect of aiding religion." He stated that appellants had acknowledged as much. In their attack upon Ohio's entire statutory scheme, they had not challenged that section which authorized publicly funded physician, nursing, dental, and optometric services in nonpublic schools.

To be sure, *Meek* had invalidated certain auxiliary services—"remedial and accelerated instruction, guidance counseling and testing, speech and hearing services"—on nonpublic school premises. But, in *Meek* the Court feared that the "publicly employed teacher or guidance counsellor" might depart from religious neutrality because he was performing important "educational services" in the church-related school. *Meek* stated, however, that Pennsylvania's provision for diagnostic speech and hearing services seemed "to fall within that class of general welfare services for children that may be provided by the State regardless of the incidental benefit that accrues to church-related schools."

The provision for diagnostic services, Mr. Justice Blackmun declared, was invalidated in *Meek* only because it was found unseverable from the unconstitutional portions of the statute.

Blackmun offered two "readily apparent" reasons why diagnostic services are different from teaching or counseling. First, diagnostic services have little or no educational content and are not closely associated with the educational mission of the nonpublic school. Secondly, the diagnostician has only limited contact with the child. The nature of the relationship "between diagnostician and the pupil", Justice Blackmun concluded, "does not provide the same opportunity for the transmission of sectarian views as attends the relationship between teacher and student or that between counselor and student." Accordingly, the Court held Ohio's diagnostic services program constitutional.

Therapeutic Services: Therapeutic psychological and speech and hearing services, guidance and counseling services, and remedial services were provided for students who had been identified as having a need for specialized attention. The services were offered, by employees of the local board of education or by personnel under contract with the state department of health, only in public schools, public centers or in mobile units located off the nonpublic school premises.

Justice Powell recognized that "unlike the diagnostician, the therapist may establish a relationship with the pupil in which there may be opportunities to transmit ideological views." *Meek* had acknowledged the danger that publicly employed personnel, providing services similar to those at issue here, "might transmit religious instruction and advance religious beliefs in their activities." In *Meek*, however, the Court emphasized that services were performed "in the pervasively sectarian atmosphere of the church-related school." The danger perceived in *Meek* "arose from the nature of the institution" in which the services were offered, and not "from the nature of the pupils." So long as the therapeutic services "are offered at truly religiously neutral locations the danger perceived in *Meek* does not arise." Accordingly, the Court held that the Ohio program had neither the impermissible effect of advancing religion nor the potential for excessive entanglement. The therapeutic services provision was constitutional.

Instructional Materials and Equipment: The Ohio statute authorized the loan to pupils or their parents of "instructional materials and instructional equipment of the kind in use in the public schools * * * and which is 'incapable of diversion to religious use.'" The equipment, e.g., projectors, tape recorders, record players, maps and globes, science kits and weather forecasting charts, was essentially the same as that provided under the Pennsylvania program which was invalidated in *Meek*. *Meek*, however, involved a program of direct loans to nonpublic schools. By contrast, under the Ohio statute the materials and equipment were loaned to the pupil or his parent. It would, however, "exalt form over substance", Justice Blackmun insisted, if such a distinction were found to justify a result different from that in *Meek*. The only difference between the two programs, he said, was the technical change in legal bailee. The instructional materials and equipment program was found to have the impermissible primary effect of providing "a direct and substantial advancement of the sectarian enterprise" of the church-related schools.

That conclusion, Justice Blackmun asserted, was compelled by Committee for Public Educ. v. Nyquist, that part of the *Nyquist* decision which invalidated New York's tuition reimbursement statute. The New York statute was invalidated despite the fact that reimbursement went to parents rather than to the church-related schools. "If a grant in cash to parents is impermissible", Justice Blackmun could not imagine "how a grant in kind of goods furthering the religious enterprise can fare any better." Indeed, he found *Nyquist* "a more difficult case than the present one." It was at least arguable in *Nyquist* that "the tuition grant did not end up in the hands of the religious schools since the parent was free to spend the grant money as he chose."

Finally, there was the perennial problem of distinguishing *Allen*'s textbook program—and Ohio's as well—from the instructional materials program. Justice Blackmun was refreshingly frank. *Allen* has remained law and it will be followed "as a matter of stare decisis." *Allen* was built upon a premise that restriction of textbook loans to those texts in use in the public schools was sufficient to ensure that the books would not be used for religious purposes. In more recent cases the Court declined to extend *Allen*'s "presumption of neutrality to other items in the lower school setting." Justice Blackmun stated that, in judging Ohio's educational materials program, he was confronted with "a choice between extension of the unique presumption created in *Allen* and continued adherence to the principles announced in our subsequent cases." He chose the latter course.

Field Trips: The statute provided for "such field trip transportation" to nonpublic school students as was provided to public school students. The parties had stipulated that the trips consisted of visits to governmental, industrial, cultural and scientific centers "designed to enrich the secular studies of students." The bus, in Justice Blackmun's view, was no more than a mobile extension of the parochial school classroom. The choice of destination was made by the nonpublic school teacher. The school controlled the timing of the trips. It was the individual teacher who made the trip meaningful. The child's instruction began with a study and discussion of the center to be visited. The dialogue continued on the bus and at the center, with the teacher pointing out items of interest and stimulating the student's imagination. And it ended with a teacher-student discussion of the experience.

Thus did Justice Blackmun describe the educational journey. *Everson's* child-safety concern could not salvage the Ohio statute. Blackmun found the field trips to be "an integral part of the educational experience", and where "the teacher works within and for a sectarian institution, an unacceptable risk of fostering of religion is an inevitable byproduct". The funding of the field trips was "an impermissible direct aid to sectarian education". Moreover, the program created "excessive entanglement", he said, because "the public school authorities will be unable adequately to insure secular use of the field trip funds without close supervision of the nonpublic teachers."

It is rather fashionable in the legal profession to speak of "landmark" cases. Were we to follow the fashion, we could certainly classify *Everson* as a landmark case in its holding and in the dicta doctrines which it established. *Lemon* could be considered a landmark, too, surely so in its impact upon elementary and secondary schools. And *Nyquist* would be at least a mini-landmark in its alternate impact. *Lemon* "landmarked" the religiously permeated parochial school and the entanglement tier of the tripartite test. In *Nyquist*, Justice Powell took to sea. He warned us that "the channel" for aid to sectarian schools "is a narrow one."

After *Nyquist* the Straits of Messina were very narrow, indeed, and implausibly perilous for the parochial schools. The sectarian navigator who escaped wreckage on Scylla's rocks was destined for disaster in Charybdis' whirlpool. A system of surveillance, necessary to restrict state aid for church-related schools to that which is secular, is entanglement according to *Lemon*. The absence of restriction, even where the aid does not flow directly to the school, is non-secular effect according to *Nyquist*.

Meek v. Pittenger and Wolman v. Walter, in their holdings, dicta and distinctions, would seem to have accurately summarized the very limited areas of permissible aid. It is confined to general governmental services such as ordinary police and fire protection, connections for water and for sewage disposal, public highways and sidewalks—the denial of which would certainly be monstrous, and destructive of the church-related schools; transportation for children to and from school; the loan of such secular textbooks as are provided in the public schools; tax exemptions for the church-related schools—a principle which inevitably follows from the approval of church tax exemptions; school lunch programs; diagnostic services performed on the nonpublic school premises; therapeutic services and remedial educational counseling services for those with special needs, provided the services are offered at a neutral site off the nonpublic school premises; standardized testing and scoring services to insure that the secular education program of the sectarian schools satisfies the state's minimal educational standards, provided the examinations are prepared by public school personnel and the grading thereof is incapable of use for religious purposes; and, by a very distinct indication in Wolman v. Walter, physician, nursing, dental and optometric services performed on the nonpublic school premises.

We have said that, in assessing legislation which provides potential aid for religious institutions, the Court has put the private elementary and secondary sectarian schools in a private category, placed them, as it were, in solitary confinement. We can be sure, however, that the parochial schools will not sit "in solemn silence in a dull, dark dock." We can be sure that proposals for aid to parochial schools and parochial school children are not a passing legislative fancy. But, faced with the *Lemon—Nyquist* alternatives, as those alternatives were advanced in Meek v. Pittenger and Wolman v. Walter, it will take the ingenious invention of an ingenious legislature, the wit of a wily Odysseus, to chart a safe passage between effect and entanglement.

(d)   The Church-Related College Cases

What appears to be an "insoluble dilemma", as Justice White termed it, for parochial elementary and secondary schools, proved no insuperable barrier for direct grants of governmental aid to sectarian institutions of higher learning. Apparently, the peril point of entanglement and nonsecular effect was passed when the parochial school student completed his twelfth grade in the parochial school.

On the day of *Lemon* the Court also dealt, in Tilton v. Richardson, with a federal program of grants for the construction of college and university academic facilities, excluding therefrom any facility used for sectarian instruction, or as a place for religious worship, or in connection with any part of the program of a school or department of divinity. All institutions, applying for grants, were required to give formal assurances that the restrictions would be respected. The United States retained a 20-year interest in any facility constructed with federal funds. If, during the 20-year period the recipient university or college violated any of the statutory restrictions, the United States was entitled to recover an amount equal to the proportion which the then value of the federal grant bore to the original cost of the facility. During the 20-year period the statutory restrictions were to be enforced by the United States Office of Education, primarily by way of on-site inspections.

Four church-related colleges and universities in Connecticut had received federal grants: Sacred Heart University for construction of a library building, Annhurst College for a music, drama and arts building, Albertus Magnus College for a language laboratory, and Fairfield University for a science building and for a library building. The Establishment challenge was addressed to the five subsidized projects at those four institutions. Chief Justice Burger wrote for the Court, sustaining the grants but invalidating that part of the statute which limited the government's interest in the covered facilities to a 20-year period.

Most of the older and, perhaps more prominent, private colleges and universities in the United States can look back upon a pious past. The spirit of Harvard's founders was inscribed on its college gates. The "schoale or colledge" at Cambridge came into being "to advance Learning and perpetuate it to Posterity; dreading to leave an illiterate Ministry to the Churches, when our present Ministers shall lie in the Dust." Noah Webster and his colleagues founded Amherst to prepare "indigent young men of piety and talents for the Christian ministry." King's College, which is now Columbia University, boasted of absolute freedom from narrow sectarianism but named five ministers of the gospel to its first board of governors. Indeed, it has been said that the courses of study in the colleges of colonial America were designed to train a class of learned men specifically for the ministry.

Most colleges and universities which began under church auspices or with religious aspirations, e. g., Harvard, Columbia, Dartmouth (which was Congregational in origin), Syracuse (sponsored by the Methodist Church), severed church affiliation or discarded religious trappings in earlier times. Others, e. g., Fordham, did so in more recent years—both old and recent converts, however, retaining their ancient religious mottoes, their chapels and chaplains for the convenience of their students, their non-indoctrinating courses in theology. Their religious beginnings are now no more than an irrelevant fact of history.

Chief Justice Burger did not deal with religious origins. He spoke of "common observation" today. But, the tone of his *Tilton* opinion suggests that the Chief Justice would agree that the overwhelming majority of private colleges and universities in the United States, including those which are church-affiliated, no longer serve the religious mission of the sponsoring church or of any church.

It is an accepted fact that, with very few exceptions, the church-related colleges and universities in the United States today cannot be profiled with the features of the church-related elementary and secondary schools of which the Court wrote in *Lemon*. Those features did not reflect, so the Court found, *Tilton*'s four Roman Catholic Church-

related colleges. It was a very important finding
of fact, indeed a crucial one. For, though sectarian use of the federally financed facilities was
prohibited by the funding statute, the statutory
restriction, standing alone, could not insure that
the federal financing had a primary secular effect.
Enforcement of the prohibition was made possible
by the fact that religion did not so permeate the
colleges that their religious and secular functions
were inseparable.

Chief Justice Burger considered both the use to
which the five federally financed buildings were
put and the character of the four church-related
colleges. The funded facilities were non-ideological
and neutral by nature. Two of the buildings were
libraries. No classes were conducted in either of
those facilities. No restrictions were imposed on
the books they acquired. The third building was a
language laboratory. It was used solely to assist
students with their pronunciation in modern for-
eign languages. The secular use of the science
building at Fairfield University and the cultural
arts building at Annhurst College seemed evident
enough to the Chief Justice. There was no evidence that religion "seeps into the use of any of
those facilities."

In the four colleges, in the facilities under consideration and in all other facilities, courses were
"taught according to the academic requirements in-
trinsic to the subject matter and the individual

teacher's concept of professional standards." All four colleges were "characterized by an atmosphere of academic freedom rather than religious indoctrination." The unrebutted findings, respecting both the character of the aided institutions and the non-religious function which the facilities served, were brief, no more than a synopsis. They were sufficient, nonetheless, to convince the Court that the federal program, insofar as it provided grants to the four Connecticut colleges for the five specified facilities, did not have the impermissible primary effect of advancing religion.

Chief Justice Burger spotted, however, one portion of the statute's enforcement provisions which was inadequate to insure that the federal aid would not advance religion. It was the provision which reserved to the government the right to recoup a proportioned amount of its grant if the subsidized facility were to be used for sectarian purposes within twenty years after completion of construction. The Court took the 20-year proviso to mean that the institution's obligation not to use the facility for sectarian instruction or religious worship expired at the end of twenty years. Obviously, substantial edifices, such as those constructed by the four Connecticut colleges, have value after that period. And, quite obviously, the unrestricted use of a valuable property, was in effect "a contribution of some value to a religious body." If at the end of twenty years the original buildings were converted into a chapel or otherwise used to promote religious interests, "the original federal grant [would] in part have the effect of advancing religion."

Since, however, the 20-year provision was not essential to the statutory program as a whole, it admitted of severance. Judicial excision of that provision alone, Burger said, would neither impair the operation or administration of the statute nor frustrate the important goals which Congress intended the legislation to serve. With the 20-year proviso expunged, the Court-restructured statute was secure under the primary effect test.

Purpose and effect having been accounted for, the Court turned to the problem of excessive entanglement. In order to determine whether government entanglement with religion is excessive, Chief Justice Burger had written in *Lemon*, the character and purposes of the aided institution, the nature of the aid, and the resulting relationship between the government and the religious authority must be ascertained. He followed that procedure in *Tilton*.

The Court stressed, as it had in its application of the effect test, the character of the aided institutions. It noted first some generally significant differences, gathered from common observation, between college and precollege education in church-affiliated institutions. College students are less impressionable and less susceptible to religious indoctrination. The skepticism of a college student is an almost impenetrable shield against any form of proselytism. College and postgraduate courses tend to curtail opportunities for sectarian influence by virtue of their own internal discipline. A high degree of academic freedom prevails at the college level, and the colleges seek to evoke free and critical responses from their students.

The Court found no evidence that *Tilton*'s four colleges varied from that pattern. Although all four were governed by Catholic religious organizations and the faculties and student bodies at each were predominantly Catholic, neither the faculties nor the student bodies were restricted to adherents of the Catholic faith. Nor were any students, including Catholic students, required to attend religious services. Theology courses were required but they were taught according to the academic requirements of the subject matter and the subject matter covered a range of human religious experiences, unconfined to Roman Catholicism. In brief, the evidence showed "institutions with admittedly religious functions but whose predominant higher education mission is to provide their students with a secular education." With colleges of that character, the Court concluded, there was little risk that religion would permeate the secular areas.

Entanglement was also lessened by the type of aid the government offered. It was nonideological and neutral by nature. Like the textbooks in *Allen* and the bus transportation in *Everson*, but unlike the teachers' services in Lemon v. Kurtzman, the federally financed facilities at the four institutions were capable of being restricted to secular purposes. And, finally, unlike the direct and continuing subsidies under *Lemon*'s Pennsylvania program, the federal aid in *Tilton* was a "one-time single purpose" construction grant.

There were, therefore, no continuing financial relationships, no annual audits, no government analyses of the institution's expenditures on religious vis-a-vis secular activities. The need for government surveillance was diminished. The need for inspection to insure that the facilities were devoted to secular instruction was minimal and hardly more than "the inspections that States impose over all private schools within the reach of compulsory education laws." Accordingly, the resulting relationship between church and government continued, as before, without excessive entanglements.

The Court also concluded that cumulatively the three factors employed in the entanglement evaluation—character of the institution, nature of the aid, resulting relationship between church and government—substantially lessened "the potential for divisive religious fragmentation in the political arena." In fact, no "continuing religious aggravation" over the federal program had been shown.

Chief Justice Burger reasoned that this might be explained by the character and diversity of the recipient colleges and universities and by the fact that they served a diverse and widely dispersed student constituency. The potential for divisiveness inherent in "the essentially local problems" of primary and secondary schools was significantly less with respect to colleges or universities.

Just as *Lemon* painted a portrait of the religiously permeated parochial elementary and secondary school, *Tilton* sketched a profile of the predominantly secular church-related college and the *Tilton* Court found on the record before it that the four Connecticut colleges conformed thereto. The profile served as a prototype in Hunt v. McNair and in Roemer v. Maryland Public Works Bd., the church-related college cases which came before the Court in 1973 and 1976 respectively. With only a minor "refinement" Mr. Justice Powell in *Hunt*, and Mr. Justice Blackmun in *Roemer*, adhered very closely to the *Tilton* analysis.

In Hunt v. McNair the challenged aid was for the construction of secular facilities on the campus of Baptist College at Charleston. Under the South Carolina scheme the construction was financed by the issuance of revenue bonds through the medium of the Educational Facilities Authority, an administrative agency established by the state legislature. In effect, the college serviced and repaid the bonds. The aid it derived was not from a state appropriation or from any form of state funding. It was derived from the low interest, resulting from its tax free status, payable on state bonds. The statute provided for the conveyance of the property or project by the college to the Authority and for a lease-back by the Authority to the college. After payment in full of the bonds the property was then to be reconveyed to the college.

To *Tilton*'s primary effect analysis Justice Powell added a modest refinement. Aid normally may be thought to have a primary effect of advancing religion, he said, "when it flows to an institution in which religion is so pervasive that a substantial portion of its functions are subsumed in the religious mission or when it funds a specifically religious activity in an otherwise substantially secular setting." The "refinement", however, would seem to have been no more than a restatement of the *Tilton* process of focusing on the character of the aided institution and the nature of the aid itself.

Although the college was subject to substantial control by its sponsoring Baptist Church, what little there was in the record established that there were no religious qualifications for faculty membership or for student admission, and that only sixty percent of the student body was Baptist, a percentage roughly equivalent to the percentage of Baptists in that area of South Carolina. There was nothing in the record to indicate that the college's operations were oriented significantly towards sectarian rather than secular education. Nor was there any evidence that the proposed transaction would provide aid to the religious activities of the college. The statute specifically excluded buildings or facilities used for religious purposes. And, it required that the lease agreement contain a clause forbidding religious use and another allowing inspections to enforce the agreement. In the absence of any countervailing evidence Justice Powell refused to assume that the statutory restrictions would not be obeyed. With those very brief observations he concluded that the implementation of the Baptist College program would not have the primary effect of advancing religion.

The entanglement aspect of the tripartite test was a little more troublesome. Though there was no evidence to demonstrate that the college was any more an instrument of religious indoctrination than were *Tilton*'s colleges and universities, and none to suggest that the inspection provision was more entangling than that in *Tilton*, the powers vested in the Authority—to fix rates, rents and fees for student use of the facilities and to establish "rules and regulations" respecting such use —posed a significant entanglement potential of a kind the *Tilton* Court had not encountered. On their face the powers seemed to provide for a continuing and intimate state supervision of the day-to-day affairs of the college. As Justice Powell read those "sweeping" powers, however, the Authority was not justified in taking action unless the college defaulted in its rental payments. In the event of default the Authority "might either foreclose on the mortgage or take a hand in the setting of rules, charges and fees." It may be argued, Powell said, that "only the former would be consistent with the Establishment Clause, but we do not have that situation before us" since no default had taken place. As thus construed, the South Carolina program passed its entanglement test.

Roemer ran true to the format of Tilton v. Richardson and Hunt v. McNair. Like the *Tilton* quartet the four recipient colleges in *Roemer* were Catholic Church-affiliated. Justice Blackmun might well have disposed of the case with a simple "see" or a nodding "accord" to *Tilton* and *Hunt.* In *Roemer*, however, the Maryland program provided for noncategorical grants and the subsidy was an annual one. *Tilton*'s subsidies were "onetime, single purpose" grants for the construction of specified secular facilities. Those formal differences required reconciliation if the Maryland program were to be sustained. Justice Blackmun did so by magnifying the character of the institutions and minimizing the form of the subsidy.

The Maryland program excluded colleges which awarded "only seminarian or theological degrees."

All other state accredited institutions of higher education were entitled to receive annually, for each full-time student (excluding those enrolled in seminarian or theological academic programs), an amount equal to 15% of the state's per-full-time-pupil appropriation for a student in the state college system. The statute specifically prohibited utilization of the funds for sectarian purposes. To insure compliance the Maryland Council for Higher Education, the state agency which administered the assistance program, required that each applicant affirm in writing that the funds would not be put to sectarian use and attach thereto a description of the specific nonsectarian uses which it planned. No change in the contemplated use could be made without the Council's approval. At the end of each fiscal year the recipient institution was required to file a report wherein the aided nonsectarian expenditures were separately identified. If the report did not adequately demonstrate that the subsidy had been used solely for secular services, the Council was authorized to undertake a "verification or audit" of the institution's financial records.

The District Court had made a very detailed analysis of the character of the four church-related colleges. It had found, as had *Tilton*, colleges with a high degree of institutional autonomy, whose student bodies and whose faculties were chosen without regard to religion, whose on-campus religious services were purely voluntary, whose academic courses and course content were untainted by religious indoctrination, and on whose campuses an atmosphere of intellectual freedom prevailed. The findings were persuasive. Justice Blackmun was convinced. The colleges were not "pervasively sectarian." The first part of *Hunt's* refinement of the secular effect standard was satisfied.

Compliance with the second part of the *Hunt* refinement came easily. *Hunt* required that the aid in fact serve only the secular side of the institution's academic endeavors. That condition was fulfilled by the statute's prohibition of sectarian uses and by enforcement of the prohibition by the Maryland Council of Higher Education. To be sure, the funds allotted were put to the use of the colleges' choice. But, no specific use was contested. Appellees had presented only a facial challenge to the statutory program. Once more the Court preferred to presume that the colleges, and the Council, would exercise their delegated control over the use of the funds in compliance with the statutory, and therefore the Constitutional, mandate.

If the Court's answer to the primary effect challenge seemed "easy", Justice Blackmun wrote, it served "to make the 'excessive entanglement' problem more difficult." The difficulty he envisioned was unduly exaggerated. The entanglement test was, in fact, satisfied with equal ease.

Tilton's three factors—character of the aided institution, form or nature of the aid, and the resulting relationship of the secular and religious authority—were very briefly canvassed. The secular character of the recipient colleges had already been established. It required no repetition. As to the form of the aid, it had been earlier noted that no particular use of state funds was before the Court. Only the "process" by which the aid was disbursed, and a use for it chosen, were in issue. Those considerations posed only "resulting relationship" problems. The resulting relationship, however, was found, in very short order, to present no grave entanglement dangers.

Tilton was distinguishable only by the form of the aid. The Maryland statute, unlike that before the Court in *Tilton*, contemplated annual decisions by the Council as to what is a "sectarian purpose", but, as the Court had already noted, "the secular and sectarian activities of the colleges are easily separated." Though "[o]ccasional audits" were possible under the Maryland statute, Justice Blackmun accepted the District Court's conclusion that they would be "quick and non-judgmental" and not likely to be any more entangling than the inspections and audits incident to the normal process of the colleges' accreditation by the state. It was true, Blackmun said, that *Tilton* favored "one-time, single-purpose" construction grants because they entailed "no continuing financial relationships or dependencies, no annual audits, and no government analysis of an institution's expenditures." It was true that the Maryland program could not claim those characteristics. But, the Court concluded, "if the question is whether this case is more like *Lemon I* or more like *Tilton*—and surely that is the fundamental question before us—the answer must be that it is more like *Tilton*."

Finally, in disposing of the "political divisiveness" appendage to the entanglement test, the Court once more tracked *Tilton*, adding only two observations, one numerical, the other a restatement of the autonomous nature of the aided institutions. The danger of divisiveness was diminished, Justice Blackmun said, by the fact that the Maryland assistance was offered to private colleges generally, more than two-thirds of which had no religious affiliation. The percentage of nonsectarian beneficiaries was "in sharp contrast to *Nyquist* * * * where 95% of the aided schools were Roman Catholic parochial schools." The church-free autonomy of the colleges was also in sharp contrast to the diocesan authority which dominated the Catholic church-related elementary and secondary schools. The independence of the colleges, it was suggested, would reduce the possibility that the Catholic Church itself, or even the religious affiliation of the schools, would become the center of political controversy.

In his parting paragraphs, Justice Blackmun could not resist, even at the risk of redundancy, return to the contrast between the character of the church-related college and that of the parochial school. For him the contrast would seem to resolve all issues: effect, entanglement, and political divisiveness as well. "Our holdings are better reconciled", he wrote, "in terms of the character of the aided institutions, found to be so dissimilar as between those considered in *Tilton* and *Hunt,* on the one hand, and those considered in *Lemon I, Nyquist* and *Levitt,* on the other." In that simple declarative sentence, Justice Blackmun reached the heart of the matter, and it was the end of the affair.

In *Lemon* it was the religiously permeated character of the Catholic parochial school which gave birth to the entanglement tier of the tripartite test. It has yet to crawl from the religious confines of the parochial school. Apart from those cases in which the Court has been called upon to resolve inter-sect ecclesiastical disputes, in no case, save a parochial school case, has a potential for excessive entanglement been found to exist. In no case, except a parochial school case, has the Court been unduly disturbed by the danger of political divisiveness. The name itself, parochial school —with the imprint of *Lemon* upon it—has produced, as it were, instantaneous entanglement.

Governmental involvement with religion or the entanglement of state and church is certainly a

Constitutionally disturbing spectacle. One may, nonetheless, question the historical credentials of the non-entanglement measures which the Court established in the parochial school cases and may wonder whether the third part of the three part test is nothing more than excess baggage.

§ 2.05   The Varieties of Entanglement

The anti-entanglement principles which the Court so artfully crafted in Lemon v. Kurtzman would appear on their face to be illustrations of judicial creativity. Neither in *Lemon*, nor in *Walz* before it, was there any reference to the annals of the First Congress which proposed the First Amendment or to any particular writings of the Founding Fathers or of those, like Madison or Jefferson, whose ample literature is said to have made "an establishment of religion" an expansive concept. The Court's omission was somewhat surprising because the anti-entanglement concept was not entirely without historical antecedents.

In *Walz*, to be sure, there was a footnote reference to Madison's Memorial and Remonstrance, and Chief Justice Burger did write of the long history of church tax exemptions which dated back to pre-Revolutionary colonial times. But the avoidance of "involvement" or of "excessive entanglement", as those not-entirely-synonymous terms were used in *Walz*, really rested upon his observation of the historical fact that in England, and in a number of colonies before our declaration of independence, the

Church of England was supported and sponsored by the crown as a state or "established" church, and that in other countries "establishment" meant sponsorship by the sovereign of the Lutheran or the Catholic Church. From that singular and simple historical premise the Chief Justice drew his conclusion that "for the men who wrote the Religion Clauses of the First Amendment the 'establishment' of a religion connoted sponsorship, financial support, and active involvement of the sovereign in religious activity." 397 U.S. at 668. "Active involvement of the sovereign", in the sense of a state-established church or a state-financed church, had, however, a fixed and finite meaning, that of a church dependent upon, and subservient to, the civil government. See Watson v. Jones, 80 U.S. (13 Wall.) at 727–728.

Walz gave "involvement" a broader meaning, perhaps one never meant at all. But *Walz* offered us very little else in the way of historical sources. Nor, for that matter, did Mr. Justice Miller in Watson v. Jones. It is somewhat strange that both Justices chose not to do so. It is still more strange that Justice Miller eschewed any mention of the Establishment Clause itself. For, if James Madison is to be our authority respecting the meaning of "an establishment of religion", *Watson*'s concept of "entanglement" was implicit in that prohibitory provision of the First Amendment. Indeed, *Watson*'s words sounded like an echo from Madison's Memorial. The suggestion that "the Civil Magistrate is a competent Judge of Religious Truth", Madison asserted, is an "arrogant pretension falsified by the contradictory opinions of Rulers in all ages and throughout the world." See Everson v. Board of Educ., 330 U.S. at 67. (Appendix to opinion of Rutledge, J., dissenting.)

In *Watson*, Mr. Justice Miller wrote of our early state and church traditions. He wrote of the "general principles" of our federal common law. "[T]he rule of action which should govern the civil courts, founded in a broad and sound view of the relations of church and state under our system of laws", Justice Miller said, "is that, whenever the questions of discipline, or of faith, or ecclesiastical rule, custom, or law have been decided by the highest * * * church judicatories to which the matter has been carried, the legal tribunals must accept such decisions as final, and as binding on them." For, it is "not to be supposed that the civil courts can be as competent in the ecclesiastical law and religious faith of all these [ecclesiastical] bodies as the ablest men in each are in reference to their own." Indeed, judicial review by the civil courts of doctrinal decisions of the church authorities would constitute "an appeal from the more learned tribunal in law which should decide the case, to one which is less so." 80 U.S. (13 Wall.) at 727, 729.

Both Chief Justice Burger, in *Walz*, and Justice Miller, in *Watson*, might have taken philosophical inspiration from several admonitions of James Madison. It was Madison's expressed belief "that both religion and government can best work to achieve their lofty aims if each is left free from the other within its respective sphere." It was Madison, the Congressional artisan of the Religion Clauses, who declared that it was best for both when there exists an "entire" abstinence "of Government from interference in any way" with the affairs of religion. IX The Writings of James Madison 487 (Gaillard Hunt, ed., 1900–1909). And, more pointedly and more forcefully, Madison asserted that the national government has "not a shadow of right * * * to intermeddle with religion." V Id. 176.

Certainly both Madison and Justice Miller captured anti-entanglement concepts, Madison in the broader sense of the separate spheres for church and state in our society, Miller in the narrower sense of judicial resolution of theological controversies. Walz v. Tax Comm'n, too, subscribed to an anti-entanglement thesis. It did so, as noted, with hardly a mention of Madison and without citation to *Watson* and the latter's lineage of cases involving church property disputes. Perhaps properly so. *Walz* presented another approach to entanglement. *Walz* set *Watson*'s and *Madison*'s non-interference themes to an anti-confrontation tune.

Walz produced a principle which dictated the avoidance of confrontations between state and church, specifically those which might arise from state taxation of churches. *Walz* did so in a context distinctly different from the ecclesiastical disputes which concerned the *Watson* Court. *Watson* wrote of synods, and schisms, and break-away sects. It wrote of the incompetence of civil courts to adjudicate matters of religious dogma or theological discipline. "The law knows no heresy", Justice Miller declared, "and is committed to the support of no dogma, the establishment of no sect." *Walz*, however, wrote of potential controversies over tax assessments, property evaluations and tax foreclosures—all civil matters which courts have the competency to adjudicate and which they customarily do resolve when the taxpayer is other than a religious entity. But, the potential evil which *Walz* envisioned was characterized as an "excessive entanglement" of government with religion. With those words it wrote the overture for *Lemon*'s orchestration of the excessive entanglement rule as the third part of the tripartite test. *Lemon* proceeded to carry the entanglement concept beyond *Walz* and far beyond *Watson*. *Lemon* wrote not of churches nor of intra-church theological disputes but of church-related schools, schools which performed the secular function of providing a secular education.

In *Lemon*'s companion case, Earley v. DiCenso, the Court characterized Rhode Island's Roman Catholic elementary and secondary schools as pervasively sectarian. In that environment, Chief

Justice Burger surmised, a teacher, teaching in a school affiliated with his or her faith, would experience "great difficulty"—a difficulty which the teachers themselves disclaimed in testimony before the trial court—in maintaining religious neutrality. There was, therefore, so the Court concluded, an intolerable risk that secular subjects would be subsumed in religious indoctrination. Nothing less than a "comprehensive, discriminating and continuing" classroom surveillance of the parochial school teacher could adequately insure against that risk. Surveillance was, in the Court's judgment, unavoidable. And any system of classroom surveillance was of the essence of entanglement.

Chief Justice Burger might well have settled for that singular test of entanglement, that inescapable, but impermissible, monitoring of the educational enterprise of the church-related elementary and secondary schools, procedures which we now call administrative entanglement. But, from *Lemon* the doctrine emerged, like the godly Roman Janus, as a two-faced creature. Its second face looked askance at the potential political controversies, the political divisiveness, which proposals for financial aid for those schools might generate.

(a) Administrative   Entanglement—and   Justice White's Critical Response

As presented in Lemon v. Kurtzman, the administrative entanglement test itself came in two parts. In addition to the entanglement inherent in that inescapable classroom surveillance, the Court found an existing entanglement in the enforcement procedures, the accounting and auditing provisions of the state statutes. The state-prescribed record keeping and financial review were designed to insure neutrality and to enable the state to ascertain, when necessary, how much of each school's expenditures were attributable to secular education and how much to religious activities. See § 2.02 (*l*), supra.

The accounting and auditing articles gave the Court no more than "concern." It might appear that those provisions were somewhat less repulsive than the ogre of surveillance, and perhaps they were. In the Court's view, nonetheless, the auditing and accounting procedures were "fraught with the sort of entanglement which the Constitution forbids." And, if by "fraught" he meant teeming or overflowing, state oversight of the financial records of the parochial schools was evidently an independent source, and an equally formidable form, of administrative entanglement. It was certainly something more than a make-weight consideration.

However objectionable any system of classroom surveillance may be or however lamentable may be the plight of the public accountant who must decipher the financial ledgers of some Mother Superior and render delicate decisions as to what pertains to the secular and what to the sectarian therein, there would appear to be something disquieting, as Mr. Justice White argued in his *DiCenso* dissent, in the process by which the *Lemon* Court arrived at its entanglement conclusions. In the *DiCenso* case the District Court had made an explicit finding that religious values did not necessarily affect the content of secular instruction in Rhode Island's parochial schools. That finding, Justice White asserted, was ignored by the Supreme Court and in place thereof the Court had substituted presumption for proof in its holding that classroom surveillance was an inescapable imperative. He also faulted the process which produced the second feature of the Court's administrative entanglement thesis. Noting that only once since the inception of the Rhode Island program had it been necessary to review school records in order to segregate expenditures for secular instruction from those for religious activities, White found very little or nothing at all in the accounting and auditing provisions provocative of any serious entanglement. The Court, in his view, had fashioned but another slender reed with which to strike down a carefully designed secular program.

Justice White was the Court's only dissenter in Earley v. DiCenso. Mr. Justice Rehnquist joined in White's concurring opinion in Roemer v. Maryland Public Works Bd. In each of those cases Justice White offered reasons of substance to reject all aspects of the Court's entanglement jurisprudence, the entire third part of the tripartite test.

As already noted, § 2.02(m), supra, in *Lemon* he found "insolubly paradoxical" a judicial logic which dictated that a state "cannot finance secular instruction if it permits religion to be taught in the same classroom; but if it exacts a promise that religion not be so taught   *   *   *   and enforces it," it is then ensnared in a web of entanglement. Five years later, in *Roemer*, he confessed that he found the Court's excessive entanglement exegesis no less "curious and mystifying" than when it was first announced.   And he insisted that both features of the administrative entanglement standard were simply superfluous.

Roemer sustained a Maryland program of financial assistance for its private church-related and non-church related colleges.   In his plurality opinion, concluding that the Maryland program did not foster an excessive entanglement, Justice Blackmun emphasized, with approval, that "the District Court gave dominant importance to the character of the aided institutions and to its finding that they are capable of separating secular and religious functions."   Yet, the same factors—the colleges were not "pervasively sectarian" and the aid in fact extended only to "the secular side" of their operations—were found to satisfy the primary effect part of the tripartite test.

Justice White's reaction was not surprising and his response is difficult to refute. The Court, by White's assessment, had focused on the same facts and findings through a different prism and had stamped the same package of facts with a different label—the one primary effect, the other entanglement. Redundancy was quite evident. Justice Blackmun came rather close to admitting as much. See § 2.04(d), supra. But, he remained defensive of the "separate" standards of effect and entanglement. He offered a one sentence reply to the Court's "redundancy" critics. "While entanglement is essentially a procedural problem", he wrote, "the primary-effect question is the substantive one of what private educational activities, by whatever procedure, may be supported by state funds." 426 U.S. at 755.

It would appear that Justice Blackmun simply produced another label for the Court's tautological essays on entanglement. The procedural-substantive distinction is undoubtedly valid. The adjective, "administrative," imports a procedural process; and a non-secular "effect," if it can be cured at all, cannot be cured by a process of administrative oversight. But the purpose served by the Blackmun dichotomy was rather obscure. Redundancy remained and the enigmatic utterances of the Court seemed to expand exponentially. For, Justice Blackmun, in applying the primary-effect test in that same paragraph of his opinion, clearly indicated that a "pervasively sectarian" institution is one in which secular activities cannot be separated from sectarian ones, and some pages later he repeated with approval the District Court's finding that the Maryland church-related colleges were not "so permeated with religion that the secular side cannot be separated from the sectarian."

"Pervasively sectarian" and "permeated with religion" were the characteristics of *Lemon*'s parochial schools. If in the lower school setting the secular side of the parochial school "cannot" be separated from the sectarian, it is most difficult to understand how state aid offered directly to those institutions can possibly escape condemnation under the primary effect test. It is, therefore, difficult to understand the need to take Constitutional inquiry further. And if the program of financial assistance for *Lemon*'s parochial schools had in fact a primary effect of advancing religion, an issue which the *Lemon* Court declined to address, then Justice Blackmun's "inseparability" doctrine certainly cast a shadow of doubt on the validity of Lemon v. Kurtzman, 411 U.S. 192 (1973) (*Lemon II*), a case which he, nonetheless, noted with approval in the final footnote of his *Roemer* opinion.

Following the Supreme Court's invalidation, in *Lemon I*, of Pennsylvania's program to reimburse nonpublic sectarian schools for their secular educational services, the District Court, on remand, enjoined payment for services rendered subsequent to

June 28, 1971, the date of the first *Lemon* decision. It permitted, however, Pennsylvania to reimburse the schools for services performed prior to the Supreme Court's decision in *Lemon I*, specifically for the educational services rendered during the 1970–71 school year. *Lemon II*'s appellants, the successful plaintiffs of *Lemon I*, challenged the limited, non-retroactive scope of the lower court's injunction. The Supreme Court, again in an opinion by Chief Justice Burger, affirmed the District Court's solely prospective application of *Lemon I.*

For the injunctive relief they now sought, *Lemon II*'s appellants resurrected the sweeping, absolutist rule of Norton v. Shelby County, 118 U.S. 425, 442 (1886), "An unconstitutional [statute] is not law; it confers no rights; it imposes no duties; it affords no protection; it creates no office; it is, in legal contemplation as inoperative as though it had never been passed." Chief Justice Burger noted that the Court had receded from the norm of *Norton* in a host of criminal cases and in other recent Constitutional decisions relating to municipal bonds. He emphasized that the trial court was vested with a broad discretionary power in shaping equity decrees and was subject to no set principle of absolute retroactivity. Equitable remedies, he said, are a special blend of what is necessary, what is fair and what is workable, and in the present case equity required a reconciliation of the Constitutional interests reflected in *Lemon I*'s "new" rule of law with the "reliance interest" which the schools had acquired under the "old." The "reconciliation" which the Chief Justice sought was to be achieved by balancing the Constitutional values at stake against the reasonableness, and the degree, of the schools' reliance upon the validity of the Pennsylvania statute prior to *Lemon I*.

Reliance was readily found and its reasonableness could not be faulted. Initially, at least, reliance was justified by the presumption of Constitutionality which attached to the Pennsylvania statute once it became law. There were weightier considerations. The Court's holding in *Lemon I* decided "an issue of first impression whose resolution was not clearly foreshadowed." Indeed, in *Lemon I* the lower court had upheld the Pennsylvania program and the Supreme Court itself had acknowledged that "we can only dimly perceive the lines of demarcation in this extraordinarily sensitive area of constitutional law." And the reasonableness of the schools' reliance was augmented by the fact that appellants had withdrawn their initial request for injunctive relief during the pendency of the *Lemon I* litigation, a tactical choice on appellants' part which might well have encouraged the schools to increase their expenditures in expectation of reimbursement by the state. Finally, the degree, or the extent, of the schools' reliance was not insignificant. It was reflected in the expenses they had incurred, and all but conceded by appellants themselves. Appellants did not dispute the fact that denial of reimbursement for services already rendered would have imposed upon the church-related schools a substantial burden which would be difficult for them to meet.

On balance the schools' reliance was found to offset "the remote possibility of constitutional harm from allowing the State to keep its bargain." What was the "constitutional harm"? Chief Justice Burger stressed the fact that the Constitutional fulcrum of *Lemon I* was excessive entanglement of church and state. The Pennsylvania statute required the Superintendent of Public Instruction to ensure that the educational services to be reimbursed were kept free of religious influences. But, under the statute the Superintendent's supervisory task "was to have been completed long ago", during the 1970–1971 school year itself, and nothing in the record suggested that the Superintendent had not faithfully executed his duties. Hence, payment of the present disputed sums compelled no further state oversight, no continuing surveillance of "the instructional processes of sectarian schools."

Two problems having "constitutional overtones" were said to remain, however. There was, first, the impact of the single and final post-audit. The post-audit, the Chief Justice stated, involved only a ministerial "cleanup" function of balancing expenditures with receipts—undertaken only once and in that setting only a minimal contact of the state with the church-related schools. Second, there was the question of infringement of the Religion Clauses by "any" payment which provides any state assistance to sectarian schools—"the issue we did not reach in Lemon I." Chief Justice Burger now disposed of that issue rather succinctly. Even assuming "a cognizable constitutional interest in barring any state payments," he said, "that interest is implicated only once under special circumstances which will not recur." And the very process of oversight, now an accomplished fact, "assures that the state funds will not be applied to any sectarian purposes."

It is certainly beyond dispute that the Constitutional evil which *Lemon I* found in the Pennsylvania program was excessive entanglement. And, without question, *Lemon I* contemplated prospective entanglements, an ongoing oversight or continuing surveillance. Taking *Lemon I* precisely as the Court decided that case, it would not make much sense—once state oversight was over and done with—to apply the *Lemon I* rule retrospectively. But two serious questions may be raised. What was the state oversight which *Lemon I* found so entangling? And did the process of oversight which *Lemon II* accepted really ensure that "state funds would not be applied to any sectarian purposes"?

Lemon I's core concern was not the entanglement arising from the review of financial records, of the courses for which reimbursement was limited, or the sectarian content of text books and instructional materials. *Lemon I* stated that classroom surveillance of the parochial school teachers themselves was inescapable and absolutely necessary to ensure that the teachers played a strictly nonideological role. The implication was rather clear that, without the policing of classroom instruction, the Court would be left with no choice but to hold that reimbursement of the schools would produce a primary effect of advancing religion or religious education. Yet, there is nothing, either in the lower court or in the Supreme Court opinions in *Lemon II*, to indicate that the Superintendent of Public Education or any state official had undertaken any classroom inspections of the parochial school teachers during the 1970-1971 school year. It would have been most surprising had any state official done so. The "new" and "unforeshadowed" rule respecting classroom surveillance came into being with the *Lemon I* decision on June 28, 1971, after the close of the 1970-1971 school year. The complete assurance which *Lemon I* sought and mandated was not to be found in *Lemon II*. Perhaps that is a roundabout way of suggesting that the Constitutional interest at stake in *Lemon I* was the Establishment Clause and not the isolated third part of the tripartite test, and that it was incumbent upon the *Lemon II* Court to address the question of whether payments for the 1970-1971 school year would have, in the absence of classroom surveillance, the impermissible effect of advancing the religious enterprise of the church-related schools.

The Court's nonretroactive application of *Lemon I* was only slightly disturbed, however, in New York v. Cathedral Academy, 434 U.S. 125 (1977), but *Lemon II* was not cast aside. *Cathedral Academy* was the sequel to Levitt v. Committee for Public Educ.

In *Levitt* a three-judge District Court, in April of 1972, had held unconstitutional a New York statute, 1970 N.Y. Laws ch. 138, which authorized reimbursement of nonpublic schools for costs incurred for state-mandated record keeping and testing services. The lower court permanently enjoined any payments under the statute, including reimbursement for expenses incurred for the last half of the 1971-1972 school year. The Supreme Court subsequently affirmed the District Court's judgment. See § 2.04(c), supra. In the interim, in June of 1972, the New York State legislature sought to temper the impact of the District Court's decree by enacting new legislation, 1972 N.Y. Laws ch. 996, which authorized reimbursement for expenses incurred prior to June 19, 1972. The new statute also conferred jurisdiction on the New York Court of Claims "to hear, audit and determine" the claims of the private schools.

The Supreme Court held the 1972 reimbursement act of the New York legislature unconstitutional.

The Court concluded that the statute would of necessity have either the primary effect of aiding religion or would result in excessive state involvement in religious affairs. Writing for the majority in New York v. Cathedral Academy, Mr. Justice Stewart distinguished *Lemon II* in several of its significant particulars.

The District Court in *Lemon II* had declined to give retrospective effect to its decree whereas the lower court in *Levitt* had expressly enjoined payments for amounts theretofore expended by the private schools. Thus, in the *Levitt* case the New York legislature had taken action inconsistent with the District Court's order when it passed the 1972 statute upon its own determination that the equities of the case demanded retroactive reimbursement. That legislative conclusion was premised upon an unacceptable assumption that "a state legislature may effectively modify a federal court's injunction whenever a balancing of constitutional equities might conceivably have justified the court's granting similar relief in the first place." Stewart disposed of the assumption with a caustic simile. Such a rule, he said, would mean that "every such unconstitutional statute [as the 1970 enactment], like every dog, gets one bite, if anyone has relied on the statute to his detriment." There was nothing in *Lemon II* to suggest such a broad general principle. Putting the importance of that distinction to the side, however, Justice Stewart emphasized that the dispositive question was whether the payments authorized by the 1972 statute offended the Religion Clauses of the First Amendment.

Unlike the Constitutional defect in the Pennsylvania program before the Court in *Lemon I*, the Constitutional invalidity of the statute before the *Levitt* Court lay in "the payment itself rather than in the process of its administration." In *Levitt* the 1970 New York statute was invalidated because there was no assurance that the lump-sum payments reflected actual expenditures for mandated services and because there was an impermissible risk of religious indoctrination inherent in the internally prepared testing for which the schools were to be compensated. Thus, the *Levitt* Court was left with no choice but to hold that the 1970 act had the impermissible primary effect of aiding religion or religious activities. The 1972 New York statute provided no more assurance than the 1970 act and the impermissible risk of religious indoctrination remained. Since the 1972 reimbursement statute authorized payments for the identical services which were to be reimbursed under the 1970 act, it was, Justice Stewart concluded, for the identical reasons invalid.

The appellee academy had asserted, however, that the 1972 reimbursement statute "required" the New York Court of Claims to review "in detail" all expenditures for which reimbursement was claimed, including all tests prepared by church-school teachers. That statutory provision, appellee argued, gave adequate, if not complete, assurance that state funds would not be used for sectarian indoctrination. The Court's response took us back to the bogs again, the inescapable bogs of entanglement, but this time with a reference to the doctrine which proscribes judicial resolution of "ecclesiastical disputes."

Justice Stewart envisioned a courtroom confrontation in which the sectarian schools would be positioned to disprove any religious content in the various classroom materials, while the state, in order to fulfill its duty to resist any possible unconstitutional payment, would be required to undertake a search for religious meaning in every classroom examination submitted in support of a claim. The ultimate evil was that the Court of Claims would then be cast "in the role of arbiter of the essentially religious dispute." That prospect, Justice Stewart declared, "of church and state litigating in court about what does or does not have religious meaning touches the very core of the constitutional guarantee against religious establishment, and it cannot be dismissed by saying it will happen only once."

In the administrative, rather than judicial, context it had happened "only once" in *Lemon II.* And there it received the Court's approval. Were there inconsistencies between the two cases? Chief

Justice Burger, who wrote the *Lemon II* syllabus, and Justice Rehnquist obviously thought so. Without elaboration they joined in a single sentence dissent to note their view that Justice Stewart had failed to apply the controlling principles established in *Lemon II.* The consistent Mr. Justice White was equally succinct. He noted his dissent "because the Court continues to misconstrue the First Amendment in a manner that discriminates against religion and is contrary to the fundamental educational needs of the country."

In *Lemon II* Chief Justice Burger observed that, since the constitutionality of the Pennsylvania program had already been settled, there was no further potential for divisive political conflict among Pennsylvania citizens and legislators respecting the desirability of that program of aid for the church-related schools. The same observation would have been pertinent, but superfluous, in *Cathedral Academy.* Indeed, it may well have been superfluous in the first place. It had questionable beginnings and it would now appear to be accorded no more than a tepid acceptance by a majority of the Court itself. The divisiveness principle deserves a brief note respecting its origin, its meaning and its significance.

(b) *Political Divisiveness*

When the Court formalized "political divisiveness" as a distinct variety of entanglement in *Lemon I,* it was "assumed" that, in a community where a large number of pupils was served by parochial schools, state assistance for those schools would generate considerable political activity. Chief Justice Burger was not pleased with the prospect of two warring political factions—the one composed of parochial school partisans, concerned with rising costs and dedicated to the religious and secular educational mission of their schools, the other comprised of those opposed to state assistance for church-related schools, whether for Constitutional, religious or fiscal reasons. The Chief Justice took it to be a fact, which could not be ignored, that most people faced with such issues would "find their votes aligned with their faith," and he declared that political division along religious lines was "one of the principal evils against which the First Amendment was intended to protect."

If "divisiveness" were a principal concern of those who conceived our Constitution or who wrote the Establishment Clause, it took a long time for the Court, or any Justice thereof, to discover it. Something akin to the divisiveness doctrine made its debut in Mr. Justice Goldberg's concurring opinion in Abington School Dist. v. Schempp. It was a rather informal introduction. Justice Goldberg suggested that the recital of prayers in public schools would so significantly involve the state in the realm of the sectarian as to give rise "to those very divisive influences and inhibitions of freedom which both religion clauses of the First Amendment preclude."

Mr. Justice Harlan was next in line with some thoughts on the topic of divisiveness. Concurring in Board of Educ. v. Allen, he repeated the Goldberg admonition but, in Harlan's view, divisiveness was not decisive. For, despite any potential for political divisiveness which might have inhered in New York's loan of textbooks to sectarian-school children, he joined in the Court's approval of the New York program. Justice Harlan returned to the subject of divisiveness in his *Walz* concurrence. Once more it was not dispositive of the challenge presented. He "entirely" subscribed to the Court's judgment which sanctioned the exemption of church properties from state taxation. He counselled, however, a wary approach to governmental programs which might incur the risk of politicizing religion. "[H]istory cautions," Harlan wrote, "that political fragmentation on sectarian lines must be guarded against." He warned that government participation "in certain programs, whose very nature is apt to entangle the state in details of administration and planning, may escalate to the point of inviting undue fragmentation."

Harlan found the makings of a divisiveness doctrine in the teachings of history and he let it stand there without elaboration. Burger was more specific in *Lemon I.* He placed the fear of divisiveness in the minds of those who proposed the First Amendment. And while he too dressed the doctrine in historical trappings, he added a quasi-modern rationalization. To have states and communities divide on the issue of state aid to church schools would, Burger wrote, "tend to obscure" other issues of apparently greater urgency. He noted that we have today "an expanding array of vexing issues, local and national, domestic and international, to debate and divide on." It would conflict with "our whole history and tradition to permit questions of the Religion Clauses to assume such importance in our legislatures and in our elections that they could divert attention from the myriad issues and problems that confront every level of government."

Burger's words seem to suggest some demeaning of religion and a second class status for those whose political decisions are dictated by their religious beliefs. But, the doctrine he fashioned is certainly not to be given so broad a sweep or so invidious a connotation. Burger put the fear of divisiveness, not the fear of God, in the mind of the First Congress. He prefaced his words with a recognition that partisan political debate and division are ordinarily normal and healthy manifestations of our democratic system of government. And the doctrine he formulated was applied in the context of governmental aid to church-related elementary and secondary schools. Only in that context has it carried any weight in the

Court's deliberations. Only in that context, so Burger surmised, would the Court "very likely" be confronted with "successive * * * and permanent annual appropriations that benefit relatively few religious groups."

Not only the free exercise of religion and a freedom from establishment, but also the right to communicate, to advocate, to assemble, to associate, to petition government was enshrined in the First Amendment. Certainly, those guarantees were not given to religiously motivated citizens in some diluted measure. The First Amendment did not cast religious partisans as pariahs in our society. Nor does it dictate to anyone, not even those who may "find their votes aligned with their faith", that he must leave his religion and moral convictions outside the voting booth.

That is to say that the divisiveness doctrine does not restrain religious groups or religious societies when they seek to persuade others to accept their views, whether religious or moral, on political issues. Nor does it interdict debate itself. It does not deny religions, the religious or religious devotees the right to state their views, however morally or religiously imbued they may be, on political issues such as divorce, abortion or birth control. The doctrine is operative only when religious groups seek governmental aid for themselves or for their institutions. But advocacy of that aid is not condemned, nor can it be, even though the advocacy be for purely religious reasons. It is government sponsorship or financial support of religious activities that is forbidden.

Thus, the divisiveness principle is a very modest one, of limited scope and limited effect. As noted, it has had no impact outside the religiously permeated precincts of the elementary and secondary parochial schools. And even though in those confines divisiveness is aggravated, as noted in *Lemon I*, "by the need for continuing annual appropriations and the likelihood of larger and larger demands as costs and populations grow," the Court ultimately acknowledged that, "while the prospect of such divisiveness may not alone warrant the invalidation of state laws that otherwise survive the careful scrutiny required by the decisions of this Court, it is certainly a 'warning signal' not to be ignored." Committee for Public Educ. v. Nyquist, 413 U.S. at 797–798.

From its somewhat shadowy "historical" beginnings as a "principal" evil against which the Establishment Clause was intended to protect, it would appear that *Nyquist* reduced the divisiveness doctrine to a shadow of itself. When we contemplate the Court's profile of the permeated parochial school, we may wonder about the need for a "warning signal." And we may wonder how scrutiny can be any more stringent than that which the Court has demanded in its parochial school cases.

[239]

§ 2.06 The Influence of History and Historical Practices

History, with its lessons taken from church-state traditions in England, in our own colonial times, and in our earliest days as a nation, has played a significant part in the Court's Establishment decisions. The religious customs of our forebears, as well as their essays, are undoubtedly instructive if we are to ascertain what the First Congress really intended when it drafted the sparse language of the Establishment and Free Exercise Clauses. Justice Black's understanding of the writings of Jefferson and Madison underscored the Establishment doctrine he formulated in *Everson*. Chief Justice Burger found the history of church tax exemptions, which were omnipresent in our colonial era and which have continued without exception throughout our national existence, persuasive support for his *Walz* decision. *Engel* documented the disruptive controversies which followed upon the various versions of the Book of Common Prayer, liturgies created by royal proclamation and approved by acts of Parliament.

Political, as well as religious, controversies followed upon *Engel* itself. *Engel* held that it was not the business of government to compose prayers, not even the "uncoerced" and non-disruptive Regents' Prayer with its bland invocation of the blessings of God upon the children, their parents, their teachers and their country. In the

[240]

Declaration of Independence Jefferson wrote of the separate and equal station to which we are entitled by "the laws of nature and of nature's God." He declared that all men "are endowed by their Creator with certain inalienable rights", and the Declaration was engrossed and signed by Jefferson and his fellow founders "with a firm reliance on the protection of Divine Providence." In compliance with a resolution adopted by the First Congress, Washington proclaimed Thanksgiving Day as a day of prayer. So, too, did John Adams. And James Madison continued the practice and turned it into a Presidential tradition. The First Congress also enacted legislation to provide for Congressional chaplaincies, a tradition which too has continued to the present day.

It would be rather difficult, therefore, to assert, in the name of Jefferson or Madison or the First Congress, that the First Amendment was intended to extirpate all vestiges of religion, all references to God or to the Creator, and all official espousal of prayer from all activities of government. An alarmed society, however, took that to be the intendment and effect of *Engel*. It was a most unpopular decision. But Justice Black was not playing the part of the village atheist. In a footnote clarification of his *Engel* holding he expressed a moderate amount of respect for our religious traditions. See § 202(g), supra. The Establishment Clause, he noted, presents no obstacle when public school children are officially encouraged to express their love of country by reciting such historical documents as the Declaration of Independence or by singing officially espoused anthems which include "the composer's profession of faith in a Supreme Being."

As an historical memorial, Jefferson's Declaration is certainly appropriate and acceptable for reading by public school children. Anthems were accepted by Black since they do not express an official position respecting religion but only the author's profession of his personal faith. Might not the latter evaluation apply as well to the uncoerced singing of traditional Christmas carols which have been sung for ages and which express not a governmental espousal but the composer's feelings for Christmas? Is the singing of carols any more a form of worship than a performance of Handel's Messiah for its musical mastery, or an exhibition of Michelangelo's Pieta for its artistic excellence or of the landscaped painting of Salisbury Cathedral for the spired architectural beauty which Constable captured? Or is the singing of traditional carols so intrinsically religious and sectarian that the Christmas spirit in public schools and at public functions must be confined to tuneful ditties about a red-nosed reindeer?

The Messiah, the Pieta and Salisbury Cathedral all have, of course, saving secular graces. And Justice Black wrote of the singing of anthems on "patriotic" or "ceremonial" occasions. Limitations may be implicit in those adjectives, but it is an historical fact that James Madison and those who sponsored the First Amendment observed Christmas as an official holiday, a day for official commemoration. And, so far as we know, the fathers of the Constitution sang carols during Christmastide. Justice Black, in turn, wrote of "anthems", or hymns of praise. He employed the plural. Whether or not Christmas carols were on Black's unpublished list of approved anthems, they have been part of our public life for over two centuries. While we do not acquire, by long usage, prescriptive rights which transcend the Constitution, it would, once more, be difficult to assert that those who wrote the Establishment Clause understood it to condemn that which they themselves practiced both before and after the First Amendment was adopted.

Tradition has branches as well as roots, but roots may provide a firmer constitutional foundation. Whatever other anthems Justice Black may have had in mind, one, at least, is rooted in history. When Francis Scott Key was inspired to write in 1814, "In God is our trust," he did more than express his personal "profession of faith in a Supreme Being." He wrote our nation's motto, a motto which is inscribed on our currency and our coins and on innumerable public buildings. That trust in God which appears on our coins and currency was approved, if only by a passing reference, in Wooley v. Maynard, 430 U.S 705, 717, n. 15 (1977). *Wooley* is but a minor illustration of the many official manifestations of a faith in God and the encouragement of prayer in our public life. There are many others to which the Court has given its dicta approval. Abington School Dist. v. Schempp, e. g., noted seven or eight examples. Justice Clark's enumeration in *Schempp* cannot be dismissed as a religious palliative prescribed by the Court to mollify religious reactions to its invalidation of prayer and Bible reading in the public schools. For, Justice Clark found his authority in the judicially unimpeachable Memorial and Remonstrance of James Madison.

"The fact that the Founding Fathers believed devotedly that there was a God and that the inalienable rights of man were rooted in Him", Clark wrote, "is clearly evidenced in their writings, from the Mayflower Compact to the Constitution itself." It is evidenced today, he said, in our public life "through the continuance in our oaths of office from the Presidency to the Alderman of the final supplication, 'So help me God.' " In that historical background, and with Madison's blessing, Justice Clark found nothing offensive to the Establishment Clause in Congressional chaplaincies or the Chaplain's prayer which opens each session of Congress, in the crier's invocation of "the grace of God" which starts each session of the Supreme

Court itself, or in the presence of federally paid Chaplains in our armed forces or the voluntary religious services for those who serve therein. Today, as in the beginning, he concluded, "our national life reflects a religious people who, in the words of Madison, are 'earnestly praying, as * * * in duty bound, that the Supreme Lawgiver of the Universe * * * guide them into every measure which may be worthy of his [blessing].' "

James Madison, as noted, also followed the Washington and Adams presidential practice of issuing prayerful Thanksgiving proclamations. In November last President Carter followed the tradition. He proclaimed Thursday, November 22, 1979 as Thanksgiving Day and asked "all Americans to give thanks on that day for the blessings Almighty God has bestowed on us." It is interesting to note that one of the last messages of President Kennedy was his Thanksgiving Proclamation of 1963, written by him shortly before that tragic November day in Dallas, and repromulgated by President Johnson upon his return to Washington.

President Kennedy's proclamation spoke of a religious heritage with roots, over three centuries old, in Virginia and Massachusetts. It recalled the proclamation of our First President in the first year of his first administration, a pronouncement which proclaimed Nov. 26, 1789 as "a day of public thanksgiving and prayer to be observed by acknowledging with grateful hearts the many signal favors of Almighty God." It spoke of President Lincoln's Thanksgiving Proclamation which sought deliverance from the "ordeal of fraternal war." It noted the nation's growing powers and pointed to the perils which accompany power. It offered thanks to God for our blessings, asked His protection against our perils and concluded "On [Thanksgiving Day] let us gather in sanctuaries dedicated to worship and in homes blessed by family affection to express our gratitude for the glorious gifts of God; and let us earnestly and humbly pray that He will continue to guide and sustain us in the great unfinished tasks of achieving peace, justice and understanding among all men and nations and of ending misery and suffering wherever they exist."

No one could ever have charged John Kennedy with ignorance of history. When he spoke of our religious heritage he knew whereof he spoke. So, we nodded and accepted this posthumous precept to gather in churches. We accepted it as something of an American tradition and those of us who sought neither sanctity nor simple peace of mind in "sanctuaries dedicated to worship" went about our business—unmolested, uncoerced. We went about our business to pray, if we wished, when we wished to pray, to play if we wished or to patch a fence or repair a rickety bicycle or poke a finger against a frozen lawn, always secure in the thought that we were doing only what we ourselves desired to do.

But, lost in the senseless tragedy of the moment and the momentous and intransient shock of the President's assassination was a larger lesson to be read in the Presidential Proclamation. Less than six months before, *Schempp* had been decided and only a year before that, Engel v. Vitale. *Engel* and *Schempp* and the President's Proclamation, each stood on different Constitutional grounds. *Schempp* condemned religious exercises, Bible readings and the recital of the Lord's Prayer, in public schools. And, however uncoerced the Regents' Prayer may be said to have been, a choice, to pray or not to pray, was compelled to be made by children who sat, with hands clasped, in the public school classroom before the dominance of the public school teacher, and the Regents' Prayer was, in the Court's view, a perversion of history. The President's Proclamation followed "the best of our traditions" and all who read the Proclamation remained free, without embarrassment, to do whatever they desired to do on Thanksgiving Day.

Quite apart from that freedom, however, the President's Proclamation was an official document. It had, as do all Presidential proclamations, historical significance. It was and is a proper subject for reading and study, without censorial expurgation of its reference to the Almighty and its espousal of prayer, in the public school classroom.

[247]

It can certainly be no more offensive to the religious or non-religious conscience than the singing of the national anthem. In each, the proclamation and the anthem, the author expressed his personal profession of faith and in neither does a public official compose a prayer.

Perhaps the larger lesson to be extracted from the contemporary promulgations of *Engel* and *Schempp* and John F. Kennedy had already been written by Justice Douglas in Zorach v. Clauson, "We are a religious people whose institutions presuppose a Supreme Being. We guarantee freedom to worship as one chooses." Justice Douglas, in what appeared to be an Establishment case, really stated a Free Exercise philosophy. Presidents with their Thanksgiving Proclamations, Congressmen with their Chaplains, the lonely soldier in the armed forces, as well as private citizens, are guaranteed religious liberty. Douglas could find no Constitutional objections to official accommodations for religious exercises.

It would be paradoxical to talk of tensions between the Establishment Clause and firmly rooted historical practices, if we mean by historical practices those which the founding fathers themselves never considered inconsistent with the interdiction of laws "respecting an establishment of religion." But, as Chief Justice Burger noted in *Walz*, there are tensions between Establishment and Free Exercise. Free Exercise guarantees are an inescapable concern in all but very evident instances of Establishment. And, conversely, the danger of Establishment is encountered when government accommodates religious practices or when conduct rooted in religious belief is exempted from regulatory statutes otherwise applicable to the public at large. More often than not, in Church-State cases the Court's ultimate judgment requires the resolution of whatever tensions may be found to exist between the two Religion Clauses of the First Amendment. To reach that resolution we must first fix the meaning of the second clause of the First Amendment, "or prohibiting the free exercise thereof."

CHAPTER THREE

THE FREE EXERCISE CLAUSE

§ 3.01 The Development of a Judicial Doctrine

The eminent master of epigram, Mr. Justice Holmes, once suggested that "a page of history" can at times be "worth a volume of logic." New York Trust Co. v. Eisner, 256 U.S. 345, 349 (1921). In Reynolds v. United States, 98 U.S. 145 (1879), the Court's first encounter with the Free Exercise Clause, Chief Justice Morrison Waite turned several pages of history to ascertain the meaning of "religion" and the scope of the Free Exercise guarantee. He marshalled the works of Madison and Jefferson, the former's Memorial and Remonstrance, the latter's bill "for establishing religious freedom" in Virginia, and the latter's letter to the Danbury Baptist Association, the same primary historical sources from which Everson extracted its Establishment pronouncements. Chief Justice Waite, however, read Free Exercise lessons therein. He focused on Jefferson's Virginia bill and the Danbury letter.

In his Virginia bill Jefferson had written that "to suffer the civil magistrate to intrude his powers in the field of opinion * * * is a dangerous fallacy" and that "it is time enough for the rightful purposes of civil government for its officers to interfere when principles break out into overt acts against peace and good order." And he advised the Danbury Baptists "that religion is a matter which lies solely between man and his God; that he owes account to none other for his faith or his worship; that the legislative powers of the government reach actions only, and not opinions." Those brief passages were all the Court needed to formulate its Free Exercise principle. Chief Justice Waite required no volume of logic.

(a) The Belief—Action Dichotomy

George Reynolds, appellant in the case of Reynolds v. United States, was a resident of the Territory of Utah. An act of Congress had made the practice of polygamy a crime in the territories of the United States. Mr. Reynolds was convicted of violating the statute. He had proved to the trial court that at the time of his second marriage he was a member of the Church of Jesus Christ of Latter Day Saints, commonly known as the Mormon Church; that he believed in its doctrines; that Mormon doctrine imposed a duty on male members, circumstances permitting, to practice polygamy; that by Mormon dogma, which he believed, the duty thus imposed was of divine origin, having been dictated by Almighty God in a revelation to Joseph Smith, the founder and prophet of the Church; and that under Mormon tenets he would be condemned to damnation in the life to come were he to refuse or fail to practice polygamy when circumstances permitted.

Joseph Reynolds had proved, in brief, that under the religious prescripts of his Mormon faith his practice of polygamy was not only permissible but obligatory. The trial judge refused to instruct the jury that it must acquit if it found that the accused had contracted his second marriage in compliance "with what he believed at the time to be a religious duty." The Supreme Court affirmed the conviction.

The question before the Court, as phrased by Chief Justice Waite, was "whether religious belief can be accepted as a justification of an overt act made criminal by the law of the land." On that issue the Chief Justice wrote for an unanimous Court. Recalling what Jefferson had written to the Danbury Baptist Association, Waite declared that "Congress was deprived of all legislative power over mere opinion, but it was left free to reach actions which were in violation of social duties or subversive of good order."

The practice of polygamy certainly implicated social duties and perhaps good order. That had been true since our pristine beginnings as a nation. And it was true in England and among the northern and western countries of Europe. From the earliest history of England polygamy had been treated as an offence against society. And Chief Justice Waite thought it specifically significant that on December 8, 1788, after passage of the Virginia act establishing religious freedom and after the Virginia convention had recommended, as an amendment to the Constitution of the United States, a declaration that "all men have an * * * inalienable right to the free exercise of religion", the Virginia legislature enacted laws making bigamy and polygamy a crime in that Commonwealth. From that day to the present, Waite stated, there never has been a time in any State of the Union "when polygamy has not been an offence against society, cognizable by the civil courts and punishable with more or less severity." Cognizant of that traditional condemnation of polygamy, the Court concluded that "it is impossible to believe that the constitutional guarantee of religious freedom was intended to prohibit legislation in respect of this most important feature of social life."

From its very nature, the Chief Justice noted, marriage is a sacred obligation, but it is also a civil contract regulated by law. Upon marriage, he observed, "society may be said to be built, and out of its fruits spring social relations and social obligations and duties, with which government is necessarily required to deal." There is no doubt that our American society has been built upon a monogamous family unit. That being so, the preservation of the monogamous family unit was a proper legislative function. Since Congress possessed the power to proscribe the practice of polygamy in the territories of the United States, the only question remaining was whether those who made polygamy a part of their religion were excepted from the operation of statute. If they were, Waite reasoned, then those who did not make polygamy a part of their religious belief could be found guilty and punished, while those who did, go free. Waite expounded:

> Laws are made for the government of actions, and while they cannot interfere with mere religious belief and opinions, they may with practices. Suppose one believed that human sacrifices were a necessary part of religious worship, would it be seriously contended that the civil government under which he lived could not interfere to prevent a sacrifice? Or if a wife religiously believed it was her duty to burn herself upon the funeral pile of her dead husband, would it be beyond the power of the civil government to prevent her carrying her belief into practice?

> So here, as a law of the organization of society under the exclusive dominion of the United States, it is provided that plural marriages shall not be allowed. Can a man excuse his practices to the contrary because of his religious belief? To permit this would be to make the professed doctrines of religious belief superior to the law of the land, and in effect

to permit every citizen to become a law unto himself. Government could exist only in name under such circumstances. 98 U.S. at 166–167.

Reynolds v. United States drew an unmistakable belief-conduct distinction, repeatedly so. It did more than that. Implicit in the distinction and in all that Chief Justice Waite wrote was a judicial doctrine which declared that Congress was free to prohibit overt acts or practices regardless of the actor's religious motives, religious convictions or religious compulsions. The Court's principle was implicit in its conclusion that Congress "was left free to reach actions which were in violation of social duties or subversive of good order." It was rather explicit in its precept that "when the offense consists of a positive act which is knowingly done, it would be dangerous to hold that the offender might escape punishment because he religiously believed that the law which he had broken ought never to have been made." 98 U.S. at 167.

Reynolds v. United States was the first of the three polygamy cases which the Mormon Church or its faithful pursued to the Supreme Court in the latter part of the last century. In Davis v. Beason, 133 U.S. 333 (1890), the Court affirmed the conviction of a Mormon who had registered and voted in the Idaho Territory in violation of a territorial law which disenfranchised those who practiced polygamy or who were members of any organization which taught, counselled or encouraged the practice. Justice Field resolved the Free Exercise issue in the light of *Reynolds*. Bigamy and polygamy, he wrote, "are crimes by the laws of the United States, and they are crimes by the laws of Idaho. They tend to destroy the purity of the marriage relations, to disturb the peace of families, to degrade woman and to debase man. * * * To call their advocacy a tenet of religion is to offend the common sense of mankind. If they are crimes, then to teach, advise and counsel their practice is to aid in their commission, and such teaching and counselling are themselves criminal and proper subjects of punishment, as aiding and abetting crime are in all other cases."

In the same year the Court sustained the constitutionality of a federal statute which abrogated the territorial charter of the Mormon Church and appropriated all Church property except that used for liturgical purposes. Mormon Church v. United States, 136 U.S. 1 (1890). Accepting Davis v. Beason as a controlling and persuasive precedent, the Court reasoned that since Congress had the authority to prohibit polygamy and to declare its practice unlawful "notwithstanding the pretence of religious conviction by which [it] may be advocated and practiced", Congress had as well the right to confiscate funds employed by the Church for the propagation of the unlawful practice.

In 1890, after three battles lost, the Mormon Church, in conference assembled, announced its surrender and formally declared its submission to the federal laws. The declaration renounced the practice of plural marriage. It noted the Mormon encounters with the Court and placed responsibility for the change upon the nation by whose laws the renunciation had been forced. The Church of Jesus Christ of Latter Day Saints then settled into a more peaceful and more profitable existence.

We were a good way into the twentieth century when the purportedly indigent but persistent Jehovah's Witnesses—once described by Professor Chafee as "a sect distinguished by great religious zeal and astonishing powers of annoyance." Z. Chafee, Free Speech in the United States 399 (1941)—began knocking on the portals of the Supreme Court as well as neighborhood doors. The Witnesses were at times as intrusive in their evangelism as they were persistent in their petitions for certiorari. They produced volumes of Free Exercise, Free Speech and Free Press decisions as they pursued their varied causes through the courts—the cause, e. g., of their zealous colporteurs who peddled their pamphlets on nightly excursions downtown in Brockton, Mass., Prince v. Massachusetts, 321 U.S. 158 (1944); the cause of their apostle who preached from his sound truck along the streets of Lockport, N.Y., Saia v. New York, 334 U.S. 558 (1948); or evangelized in a public park in Pawtucket, R.I., Fowler v. Rhode Island, 345 U.S. 67 (1953); or carried his preaching and proselyting to his neighbor's doorstep, Martin v. City of Struthers, 319 U.S. 141 (1943). The first judical landmark for Jehovah's Witnesses was, however, Cantwell v. Connecticut, 310 U.S. 296 (1940), the case in which the Court first held that the Free Exercise guarantee was applicable to the states perforce of the Fourteenth Amendment.

(b) The Transition Period

Newton Cantwell and his sons, Jesse and Russell, professed to be ordained ministers of Jehovah's Witnesses. Their journey to the Supreme Court began with their arrest on Cassius Street in New Haven, a densely populated neighborhood where ninety per cent of the residents were Roman Catholics. The Cantwells had engaged in the unlicensed door to door solicitation of contributions for their religious cause. It was also their practice to play phonograph records, on Cassius Street corners, which purported to expound the message of Jehovah. The message was patently offensive to those who paused to listen. It vilified Roman Catholics and attacked all organized religious systems, particularly the Catholic Church, as instruments of Satan.

The Connecticut Supreme Court sustained the conviction of all three defendants under a state statute which prohibited the solicitation of money or other items of value for any alleged religious or charitable cause "unless such cause shall have been approved by the secretary of the public welfare council." The council secretary was vested with authority to determine whether the cause asserted was or was not a religious one. Jesse Cantwell was also convicted under a count alleging breach of peace. That conviction, too, was affirmed by the state's Supreme Court. The Supreme Court of the United States reversed on all counts.

In voiding the breach of peace conviction, Mr. Justice Roberts adopted the free speech test which had first been formulated by Justice Holmes in Schenck v. United States, 249 U.S. 47 (1919). There was no evidence of a "clear and present danger" to the state's conceded interest in public safety, peace or order which could justify the suppression of religious views that simply annoyed, or even angered listeners. In the realm of religious faith, Justice Roberts observed, as well as in the political arena, sharp differences of opinion inevitably arise. And in both fields the pleader may at times resort to exaggeration, to vilifications and to false statements. But, the liberty to do so, the Court concluded, despite excesses and abuses, is in the long view "essential to enlightened opinion on the part of the citizens of a democracy."

Justice Roberts' assessment of the solicitation statute was almost exclusively an assessment of the Free Exercise guarantee, even though he had apparent free speech and free press precedents by which he might have voided the Connecticut statute on its face. The press and speech precedents had been established in two other Jehovah's Witness cases, Lovell v. City of Griffin, 303 U.S. 444 (1938) and Schneider v. State, 308 U.S. 147 (1939).

Lovell was the first Witness case to be accorded a full hearing by the Supreme Court. It invalidated, on its face, a municipal ordinance of the City of Griffin, Georgia, which prohibited the distribution of circulars, handbooks or literature of any kind on the streets of the metropolis without first obtaining a permit from the city manager. The statute was also comprehensive with respect to the method of "publication" and unlimited as to the time or place of distribution. Alma Lovell had distributed pamphlets, on the streets of Griffin, setting forth the gospel of the "Kingdom of Jehovah." She had not applied for the required permit. She had declined to do so, she said, because she regarded herself as sent "by Jehovah to do his work" and an application for a permit would have been "an act of disobedience to His commandment." Alma Lovell asserted free exercise, free speech and free press protections. The Court confined its holding to the free press guarantee. The ordinance was simply too broad in its sweep and its enforcement was left to official discretion. A statute of that character, the Court concluded, "strikes at the very foundation of the freedom of the press by subjecting it to license and censorship."

Schneider v. State voided a similar ordinance of the Town of Irvington, N. J. which required a license from the chief of police to canvass, solicit, distribute circulars or call from house to house within the township. Miss Schneider's door to door canvassing on behalf of the Watch Tower Bible and Tract Society, certified by the Society to be one of Jehovah's Witnesses, was hardly any different than the solicitation in which the Cantwells engaged. The Court's invalidation of the Irvington ordinance rested on the First Amendment's Free Speech and Free Press Clauses. Once more the Court observed that pamphlets have proved most effective instruments in the dissemination of opinion. Again, the broad scope of the statute and the degree of discretion given to the chief of police created what was tantamount to a system of censorship. And, once more, the Court concluded that to require "a censorship through license which makes impossible the free and unhampered distribution of pamphlets strikes at the very heart" of the free speech and free press guarantees.

It was not until *Cantwell* that the Court employeed the Free Exercise Clause to justify its position in licensing cases. Justice Roberts had a compelling reason to do so. By the express terms of the statute a state official was authorized to adjudge whether the cause for which the Cantwells solicited contributions was a religious one. Roberts cited *Reynolds* and Davis v. Beason with approval, but he turned *Reynolds'* conduct—belief dichotomy several degrees from the point at which Chief Jus-

tice Waite had compassed it. He wrote more solic-
itously of religion-based conduct. He wrote what
is, perhaps, the most frequently cited passage on
the scope of the Free Exercise Clause.

> The constitutional inhibition of legislation on
> the subject of religion has a double aspect.
> On the one hand, it forestalls compulsion by
> law of the acceptance of any creed or the prac-
> tice of any form of worship. Freedom of cons-
> cience and freedom to adhere to such religious
> organization or form of worship as the individ-
> ual may choose cannot be restricted by law.
> On the other hand, it safeguards the free ex-
> ercise of the chosen form of religion. Thus
> the Amendment embraces two concepts,—free-
> dom to believe and freedom to act. The first
> is absolute but, in the nature of things, the
> second cannot be. Conduct remains subject to
> regulation for the protection of society. The
> freedom to act must have appropriate defini-
> tion to preserve the enforcement of that pro-
> tection. In every case the power to regulate
> must be so exercised as not, in attaining a
> permissible end, unduly to infringe the pro-
> tected freedom. No one would contest the
> proposition that a State may not, by statute,
> wholly deny the right to preach or to dis-
> seminate religious views. Plainly such a pre-
> vious and absolute restraint would violate the
> terms of the guarantee. It is equally clear
> that a State may by general and non-dis-

criminatory legislation regulate the times, the places, and the manner of soliciting upon its streets, and of holding meetings thereon; and may in other respects safeguard the peace, good order and comfort of the community, without unconstitutionally invading the liberties protected by the Fourteenth Amendment. The appellants are right in their insistence that the Act in question is not such a regulation. If a certificate is procured, solicitation is permitted without restraint but, in the absence of a certificate, solicitation is altogether prohibited. 310 U.S. at 303–304.

The Court's conclusion had the sound of the antientanglement concept which had been conceived in Watson v. Jones and which was later to be formulated as the third part of the *Lemon I*'s Establishment test. Justice Roberts wrote, "[T]o condition the solicitation of aid for the perpetuation of religious views or systems upon a license, the grant of which rests in the exercise of a determination by state authority as to what is a religious cause, is to lay a forbidden burden upon the exercise of liberty protected by the Constitution."

Though *Cantwell* had exalted religious belief to the highest Constitutional altar and though Justice Roberts had professed judicial concern for religion-based conduct, the Court, only two weeks after the *Cantwell* decision, found very little Constitutional protection for conduct compelled by religious belief. Minersville School Dist. v. Gobitis, 310 U.S. 586 (1940) sanctioned the expulsion of two children, Jehovah's Witnesses, from public elementary school, who, because of their religious conviction that it was a graven image, refused to salute the American flag. Lillian and Walter Gobitis asserted more than a conviction. Their conduct was compelled, they alleged, by the dictates of their religion. For, to salute the flag would ascribe salvation to it rather than to Jehovah, who alone had the power to save souls.

The Court declined the invitation to sit as a super-school-board to reassess school policies adopted by local school officials. It could find no fault with the local authorities who had in their reasoned and reasonable judgment chosen the compulsory flag salute to promote patriotism and the national unity which are at the heart of national security. It is true, Justice Frankfurter added, that judicial review is a fundamental part of our constitutional scheme but "to the legislature no less than the courts is committed the guardianship of deeply-cherished liberties." Justice Stone dissented. The very essence of liberty, he wrote, is freedom from compulsion as to what one shall think or what he shall say, "at least where the compulsion is to bear false witness to his religion." He demanded careful scrutiny "of legislative efforts to secure conformity of belief and opinion by a compulsory affirmation of the desired belief."

Patriotic emotions might well have been aroused by the *Gobitis* dissent. But, if the freedom to believe what one chooses to believe is absolute, as *Cantwell* said it was, Justice Stone's opinion, though he alone dissented, could not be long ignored. For, the *Gobitis* Court was really not presented with a prohibition of conduct, such as the practice of polygamy which the state may prohibit because it debases man, degrades woman and disturbs the peace of families. What was essentially involved in *Gobitis* was the imposition of belief. Minersville School District v. Gobitis was short lived. Three years later it was overruled in West Virginia State Board of Educ. v. Barnette, 319 U.S. 624 (1943). Mr. Justice Jackson wrote for the majority of the Court.

On its facts *Barnette* was *Gobitis* revisited. The compulsory patriotic exercise of saluting the American flag was required of children in the elementary grades of the public schools in West Virginia. The penalty for refusal was expulsion and parents were subject to criminal prosecution if their children failed to attend school in compliance with the state's compulsory education laws. The suit was instituted by Walter Barnette, on behalf of his children, Jehovah's Witnesses, who because of their belief could not comply with the flag salute prescription without violating the tenets of their religion. Walter Barnette's claim was a Free Exercise claim. Expulsion of his children for failure to comply, he argued, was a denial of his and their religious liberty.

Justice Jackson put the issue in a word with broader connotations than "religious" liberty. "Here," he wrote, "we are dealing with a compulsion of students to declare a belief." Certainly, "belief" encompasses a variety of concepts, political, economic, social, moral as well as religious. Nor did Justice Jackson deal with conduct per se. For him the flag salute was a form of utterance. "Symbolism," he noted, "is a primitive but effective way of communicating ideas." He wrote not of Free Exercise alone but of all the freedoms found in the First Amendment and he imposed a test more strict than any suggested in the Court's prior Free Exercise decisions. The right of a state to regulate, for example, a public utility might well include, he said, the power to impose whatever restrictions a legislature may have a rational basis for adopting. "But, freedoms of speech and of press, of assembly, and of worship may not be infringed on such slender grounds. They are susceptible of restriction only to prevent grave and immediate danger to interests which the State may lawfully protect."

Jackson concluded that "the action of the local authorities in compelling the flag salute and pledge transcends constitutional limitations on their power and invades the sphere of intellect and spirit which it is the purpose of the First Amendment

* * * to reserve from all official control." He prefaced his conclusion with his famous "fixed star."

> If there is any fixed star in our constitutional constellation, it is that no official, high or petty, can prescribe what should be orthodox in politics, nationalism, religion, or other matters of opinion or force citizens to confess by word or act their faith therein. If there are any circumstances which permit an exception, they do not now occur to us. 319 U.S. at 642.

A little more than seven months after the *Barnette* decision the Court reviewed another episode in the recurring controversies between Jehovah's Witnesses and state authorities. But this time, Prince v. Massachusetts, the Court dealt exclusively with the Free Exercise Clause.

Sarah Prince was the guardian of a nine year old girl. Both guardian and ward were Jehovah's Witnesses. A Massachusetts statute prohibited the sale, or the offer to sell, any merchandise of any description in any street or public place by a boy under the age of twelve or by a girl under the age of eighteen. A second statute made it a criminal offense for any parent or guardian to permit such minors in his or her custody to engage in the prohibited selling or solicitation. Sarah Prince and her nine year old ward had offered their religious tracts for sale on the streets of Brockton, Mass. At her trial Sarah Prince offered testimony to show that her ward believed it was her religious duty to engage in that public activity and that her failure to do so would bring condemnation "to everlasting destruction at Armageddon." The testimony was excluded. Sarah's conviction was sustained by the Supreme Court.

Justice Rutledge, speaking for the majority, held that the state's concern for the health and well-rounded growth of young people and its interest in protecting them against the "crippling effects of child employment, more especially in public places, and the possible harms arising from other activities subject to all the diverse influences of the street" outweighed both the claim based on religious freedom and that grounded on parental rights respecting the custody and care of children. Mr. Justice Murphy, dissenting, was caustically critical of the Court's "vague references to the reasonableness underlying child labor legislation in general." Only proof of a grave and immediate danger to the state or to the health, welfare or morals of the child, he argued, would warrant the restriction on the child's right to practice her religion. The state, in Murphy's view, had completely failed to provide that proof.

Cantwell was a licensing case. In *Barnette* the state had sought to compel the affirmative profession of a belief. *Prince* presented a different issue. The petitioner and her ward had sought exemption, on religious grounds, from child labor laws of general application. *Prince* gave its approval to *Reynolds* and Davis v. Beason. And *Reynolds* had refused to permit the punishment of those who did not make polygamy a part of their religious belief, while those who did, went free. When government exempts individuals from compliance with law solely on the basis of religious belief, does it follow that government is subjecting others to its penalties and punishments for their failure to subscribe to those same beliefs? If it does, we are embroiled with the Establishment Clause as well as the Free Exercise of Religion. And that question really poses two others: (1) when may government exempt religion-rooted or religion-based conduct from general regulatory statutes without transgressing the Establishment Clause?; and (2) when does the guaranty of religious liberty compel exemption from doing what government deems necessary for the common good, or from a penalty for conduct which appears dangerous to the general welfare? *Prince* denied an exemption but it did not answer those "may" and "must" questions. Answers began to emerge in Braunfeld v. Brown, but *Braunfeld* did little more than scratch the surface of the underlying issues.

(c) *The Modern Approach*

In Braunfeld v. Brown, one aspect of which has already been noted along with McGowan v. Maryland, supra, § 204(b), the Court held that the Free Exercise Clause did not mandate a Sunday Closing

Law exemption for Orthodox Jewish merchants who observed Saturday as the Sabbath. They were, as a result, required to close shop two days a week—on Saturday by reason of their religious beliefs, on Sunday perforce of the state statute. *Braunfeld* was not *Reynolds* revisited. Nor was it Prince v. Massachusetts. In *Reynolds*, the Mormon faith imposed a "duty" upon male members to practice polygamy and in *Prince* the faith of Jehovah's Witnesses imposed a "duty" upon its adherents, minors included, to solicit the sale of religious pamphlets in public places. In those cases religious practice themselves were subjected to criminal sanctions. But the Orthodox Jewish faith imposed no duty upon its faithful to engage in Sunday labor. The *Prince* and *Reynolds* holdings made it clear that legislation which penalizes a religious practice is not per se violative of the Free Exercise Clause. The *Braunfeld* logic suggested that, if the state can impose a direct burden on religious practices, presumably a higher degree of coercion, it can impose a lesser degree.

In his plurality opinion Chief Justice Warren emphasized that the Sunday laws did not make unlawful any religious practices of the appellants. As applied to them the laws did no more than add an economic burden. What they were certain to lose, if faithful to their religious beliefs, was the opportunity to merchandize six days a week. But that apparent economic disadvantage, Warren said, was "only an indirect burden." He stated his rule in a single sentence, "[I]f the State regulates conduct by enacting a general law within its power, the purpose and effect of which is to advance the State's secular goals, the statute is valid despite its indirect burden on religious observance unless the State may accomplish its purpose by means which do not impose such a burden." The alternative means had already been canvassed, and found ineffective to accomplish the state's legitimate secular goals, in McGowan v. Maryland, supra, §§ 2.03, 2.04(b).

The *Braunfeld* appellants, however, proposed another alternative available to the state—an exception from the Sunday proscription for those who, because of religious conviction, observe a day of rest other than Sunday. Warren noted several difficulties in the exemption claim. For one, there was the enforcement burden thrust upon the state, the burden of policing compliance two or more days a week rather than one. There was the inescapable element of human frailty, the temptation for some to improvise religious convictions in order to close shop on a less profitable day and thus to gain the advantage of a Sunday seller's market. Those suspect claims, in turn, raised the spectre of Constitutionally offensive state-conducted inquiries into the sincerity of individual religious beliefs. Nonetheless, the Chief Justice noted that a number of states provided exemptions for those who observed a Sabbath other than Sunday, and he added that "this may well be the wiser solution to the problem."

Of course, if we ponder over all of the Court's ruminations on the tripartite test of Establishment, an exemption provision would on its face suggest a solely religious purpose; it might produce a non-secular effect, and in conjunction with the non-secularity of purpose and effect there could be entanglements by government with unknown or discrete minority religions, if the state were to conduct inquiry into the sincerity of an individual's religious belief. We are brought back then to the question: when "may" the state exempt religion-rooted or religion-based conduct from general regulatory statutes without offending the Establishment Clause? Warren gave no absolute answer. He simply suggested that exemption may well be "the wiser solution."

One year later Warren's "wiser solution" became law, adjudicated by an "appeal dismissed" in Commonwealth v. Arlan's Dept. Store, 357 S.W.2d 708 (Ct.Appeals, Ky.), appeal dismissed sub nom. Arlan's Dept. Store v. Kentucky, 371 U.S. 218 (1962). The Kentucky legislature had done what Warren thought it was wise to do. Rejecting an Establishment Clause challenge by Sunday observers, the Kentucky Court of Appeals held that the exemption "did not affirmatively prefer any religion nor amount to the establishment of a religion." Rather, it simply avoided "penalizing economically the person who conscientiously observed a Sabbath other than Sunday." The state court offered no analysis except to suggest that exemptions were upheld by implication in Warren's "wiser solution."

An appeal dismissed by the Supreme Court carries the persuasion of stare decisis. But, whatever may be the attributes of stare decisis, the "may" question is wholly resolved when the circumstances of a particular case dictate that the state "must" grant exemption to comply with the Free Exercise Clause. For, we then give the Free Exercise Clause a preferred position, and have necessarily disposed of Establishment concerns. Mr. Justice Brennan found those circumstances in Sherbert v. Verner, 374 U.S. 398 (1963).

Adele Sherbert was a member of the Seventh-Day Adventist Church. She was discharged by her employer because she refused to work on Saturday, the Sabbath day of her faith. Her claim for unemployment compensation benefits under the South Carolina compensation act was denied under a statutory provision which rendered ineligible for benefits a claimant who failed, without good cause, to accept available suitable work when offered him. The compensation commission found that Adele Sherbert's restriction upon her availability for Saturday work brought her within the ineligibility clause. Its finding was affirmed by the

South Carolina Supreme Court. The state court rejected appellant's contention that, as applied to her, the disqualifying provisions of the statute abridged her right to the free exercise of her religion. The Supreme Court of the United States, with only two dissents, reversed.

If the decision of the South Carolina Supreme Court was to withstand appellant's Constitutional challenge, Justice Brennan ruled, "it must be either because her disqualification as a beneficiary represents no infringement by the State of her constitutional rights of free exercise, or because any incidental burden on the free exercise of appellant's religion may be justified by a 'compelling state interest in the regulation of a subject within the State's constitutional power to regulate.' "

First, the disqualification was held to impose a burden on the free exercise of appellant's religion. It was an indirect burden. No criminal sanction compelled Adele Sherbert to work on her Sabbath day. But, the disqualification derived solely from the practice of her religion and, in the Court's view, the pressure upon her to forego that practice was unmistakable. She was compelled "to choose", Brennan said, "between following the precepts of her religion and forfeiting benefits, on the one hand, and abandoning one of the precepts of her religion in order to accept work, on the other hand." The imposition of such a choice, he concluded, "puts the same kind of burden upon the free exercise of religion as would a fine imposed against appellant for her Saturday worship." Second, no compelling interest had been demonstrated by the state to justify "the substantial infringement" of appellant's First Amendment right. The state had suggested no more than the bare possibility that fraudulent claims might dilute the compensation fund and, even if there were a demonstrable danger of spurious claims, "it would plainly be incumbent upon appellees to demonstrate that no alternative forms of regulation would combat such abuses without infringing First Amendment rights."

The test which Justice Brennan formulated was not a balancing test, although the Court had often characterized it as such. It was a two step test which tells us what the adverse parties, individual and state, must prove. The individual claimant must show that the challenged regulation imposes some significant burden on the free exercise of his or her religion. Once the burden is shown, it is incumbent upon the state to demonstrate that the regulation, or denial of exemption, is "necessary" for the promotion or protection of a "compelling" state interest. Quite obviously, the *Sherbert* rationale turned the *Reynolds'* doctrine 180 degrees. Belief remained absolute but practices received a protection which not only *Reynolds*, but *Prince* and *Braunfeld* as well, denied them.

Nevertheless, only principles, not the results, of *Braunfeld*, *Prince* and *Reynolds* were restated.

Justice Brennan, in fact, undertook to distinguish *Braunfeld.* He tallied up differences. He spoke of the enforcement burdens present in *Braunfeld,* the prospect of fraudulent religious claims asserted for competitive commercial advantages, and the potential entanglements between state and church, all of which Chief Justice Warren had enumerated in *Braunfeld* without use of the word, "compelling." Brennan stated that in *Braunfeld* exemptions for Sabbatarians "appeared" to present an administrative burden of such magnitude as to render the entire statutory scheme unworkable. Mr. Justice Brennan had to be talking with civil tongue in cheek. In *Sherbert* he discarded *Braunfeld*'s direct-indirect dichotomy. And he had dissented in *Braunfeld* because the Court's decision did not conform to his compelling interest standard, the precise test he applied with majority acceptance in *Sherbert.* In *Braunfeld* he would have mandated an exemption for Sabbatarians. In *Sherbert* he did. *Braunfeld* stands unreversed but its viability is unpredictable.

Wisconsin v. Yoder, 406 U.S. 205 (1972), was the third case in the modern triology of Free Exercise cases. *Yoder* held that the state could not penalize Amish parents who, by reason of religious convictions, refused to send their children to public or private schools beyond the eighth grade. The Amish practice was in contravention of Wisconsin law which required school attendance until the age of sixteen. Writing for the Court, Chief Justice

Burger apparently rephrased the *Sherbert* rationale, but without reference to "alternate means," which might accomplish what the state sought to accomplish without infringing religious liberty. For a state "to compel school attendance beyond the eighth grade against a claim that such attendance interferes with the practice of a legitimate religious belief," Burger stated, "it must appear either that the State does not deny the free exercise of religious belief by its requirement, or that there is a state interest of sufficient magnitude to override the interest claiming protection under the Free Exercise Clause." He added that "only those interests of the highest order and those not otherwise served can overbalance legitimate claims to the free exercise of religion."

Burger called his restatement a "balancing process" and he never used the term, "compelling state interest" or the adjective, "necessary", the second feature of Brennan's compelling interest requirement. In its application, however, there was no discernible difference between Burger's balancing process and *Sherbert*'s two-step test. If there be a difference between a "compelling" state interest and interests of an overriding "magnitude" or those "of the highest order," it is only a semantical difference, dependent upon the preference of different Justices for different adjectives which have essentially the same meaning. And before the *Yoder* Court concluded its case it did find that the denial of an Amish exemption was not necessary for the accomplishment of the state's conceded interest in child education.

The interests of the state and those of the Amish respondents coincided with respect to private or public elementary school education. Their interests parted with respect to the two years of post-primary formal education required by the state. The record established, however, that the Amish practice of providing personal vocational training for their children in their rural communities was religiously rooted in an ancient religious heritage. Their religious practice was concededly sincere. And the Amish respondents had given ample evidence that compliance with the compulsory formal education law beyond the eighth grade would gravely endanger the survival of their sect. The Amish had proved substantially more than a significant burden on the free exercise of their religion. Under the Court's balancing process, then, the Amish burden had to be counterbalanced with the state's countervailing interests.

The state contended that its system of compulsory education was sufficiently "compelling," the *Sherbert* adjective, to require subordination of the Amish religious practice. The purpose served by the compulsory education law, Burger stated, was that of preparing citizens for effective, intelligent, self-reliant and self-sufficient participation in social and political affairs. That interest, however, was substantially served by eight years of formal primary school training supplemented by the Amish program of informal vocational training after completion of the eighth grade. The Amish respondents had established, Burger concluded, that "the Amish alternative" to formal secondary education was capable of fulfilling the social and political responsibilities of citizenship "without compelled attendance beyond the eighth grade at the price of jeopardizing their free exercise of religious belief." Chief Justice Burger had already acknowledged that education is a "paramount" responsibility of the state. Might we not, then, resort to the *Sherbert* rationale and note that the Amish alternative had also established that the denial of an Amish exemption was not "necessary" for the promotion of that "paramount" interest of overriding "magnitude" which the state sought to promote by its compulsory school attendance laws?

Sherbert v. Verner set the Free Exercise Clause on a very high pedestal. *Yoder*, when combined with *Sherbert*, gave it a preeminence it had never known before. It had been said in Brown v. Board of Educ., 347 U.S. 483 (1954), the Court's landmark desegregation case, that "education is perhaps the most important function of state and local governments" and that "compulsory school attendance laws * * * demonstrate * * * the im-

portance of education to our democratic society."
In *Yoder*, Chief Justice Burger declared that the
providing of public schools "ranks at the very apex
of the functions of a state." Certainly, then, if the
state "must" grant exemption from compulsory
school attendance laws out of deference to religious
practices, the Free Exercise Clause may well be
the brightest of the "fixed stars" in our Constitutional constellation.

(d) Belief and Conduct Distinguished

If, in *Sherbert* and *Yoder*, the Supreme Court
elevated the Free Exercise Clause to a preferred
position among First Amendment guarantees, religious beliefs must be supremely supreme. *Sherbert* and *Yoder* dealt with religion-based conduct.
And both acknowledged that "belief", in *Cantwell*'s
renowned statement, was absolute. Of course, belief can be known only by its profession. And
though profession, by definition, involves an act, it
is necessarily the profession of belief which is
absolute. For, compelled profession, Justice Jackson wrote in West Virginia State Board of Educ.
v. Barnette, invades "the sphere of intellect and
spirit."

Torcaso v. Watkins, therefore, was a genuine
Free Exercise case which paid the majestical deference due to religious belief. *Torcaso*, with an un-
usual Court unanimity, held unconstitutional a
Maryland statute which required its citizens to

swear a belief in God in order to obtain a commission as a notary public. *Cantwell's* absolute freedom of belief was created for a case like *Torcaso.* The Maryland statute compelled the profession of a belief in God under pain of forfeiture of a state office. And, since belief is absolute, there was no need to evaluate state interests which might justify the state statute.

Mr. Justice Black wrote the Court's opinion in *Torcaso.* He was the author of *Everson.* In his *Everson* enumeration of Establishment Clause prohibitions he had written, "Neither a state nor the Federal Government * * * can pass laws which aid one religion, aid all religions, or prefer one religion over another. Neither can force [a person] to profess a belief or disbelief in any religion." *Torcaso's* Maryland statute had preferred "all religions" over non-religion and, since there are religions which do not teach what would generally be considered a belief in God, e. g., Buddhism, Taoism, Ethical Culture, Secular Humanism and others, it had preferred some religions over other religions. Finally, it had forced the profession of a belief in God-centered religions. The Court's *Torcaso* decision was firmly rooted in *Cantwell's* "belief" autonomy and it held firm footing in three of *Everson's* Establishment Clause proscriptions. The Maryland statute violated both Religion Clauses of the First Amendment. The Court so held.

The Supreme Court returned to *Torcaso* in McDaniel v. Paty, 435 U.S. 618 (1978). The *McDaniel* Court was unanimous in invalidating a Tennessee statute which barred "ministers of the gospel, or priest[s] of any denominations whatever" from serving as delegates to the State's constitutional convention. Four opinions were offered by the Court but none commanded majority acceptance. Once more it was the opposing views of Chief Justice Burger and Justice Brennan which required evaluation. Justices Powell, Rehnquist and Stevens joined in the opinion of the Chief Justice, while Justice Marshall joined in the Brennan opinion. The question they raised was that of defining belief, of determining where belief ends and conduct begins.

Chief Justice Burger stated that the Tennessee disqualification operated against appellant because of his "status" as a "minister" or "priest", and ministerial status was defined by the state court in terms of conduct and activity. The Tennessee court had held that the disqualification reached those dedicated to the full time "promotion" of the religious objectives of a particular religious sect and it had defined "priest" as one who "performs" ritualistic and other ministerial functions. Thus, in Burger's view the Tennessee disqualification was directed primarily at "status, acts and conduct" and it was, therefore, unlike the requirement in *Torcaso* which focused on "belief." Hence, "the

Free Exercise Clause's absolute prohibition of infringements on the 'freedom to believe' is inapposite here."

The infringement on appellant's religiously based activities could be justified, therefore, only by proof of state interests of the highest order. The rationale of the Tennessee restriction, Burger said, was that ministers elected to public office would necessarily exercise their powers to promote the interests of one sect or thwart the interest of another contrary to the antiestablishment principle which commands neutrality. The Chief Justice found "no persuasive support for the fear that clergymen in public office will be less careful of antiestablishment interests or less faithful to their oaths of civil office than their unordained counterparts." In the absence of proof of an overriding state interest the disqualification statute was declared unconstitutional.

Justice Brennan followed *Torcaso.* For him it was controlling both in its Free Exercise rationale and in its Establishment pronouncements. In his view, balancing was a needless exercise. He rejected the foundation stone on which Burger's balancing process was built, the Burger idea that clerical status was defined in terms of conduct and that the Tennessee proscription related only to acts, and not belief. For Brennan, McDaniel v. Paty was a bona fide "belief" case. The priesthood and the ministry were professions of belief, symbolic manifestations of an intense and sincere dedication to religious convictions. The Tennessee disqualification was as burdensome a penalty on a profession of belief as was Maryland's test oath in *Torcaso*. And, as in *Torcaso*, so in *McDaniel* freedom to believe was absolute.

"One's religious belief", Justice Brennan wrote, "surely does not cease to enjoy the protection of the First Amendment when held with such depth of sincerity as to impel one to join the ministry." The Tennessee law, he said, imposed "a unique disability upon those who exhibit a defined level of intensity of involvement in protected religious activity." A test for office based upon religious convictions, he declared, is no different than one based on denominational preference and a law "which limits political participation to those who eschew prayer, public worship or the ministry as much establishes a religious test as one which disqualifies Catholics, or Jews, or Protestants." *Torcaso* condemned the policy of probing religious beliefs by test oaths or of limiting public office to persons who have particular religious beliefs. Justice Brennan concluded, therefore, that the principle of *Torcaso* equally condemned the religious qualification for elective office imposed by Tennessee.

Justice Brennan's holding gave the fullest measure of protection to appellant's Free Exercise claim but his thesis had a more expansive potential.

Justice Roberts stated a truism in his *Cantwell* declaration that belief is absolute. So, too, did Justice Black in *Torcaso,* when he condemned the "policy of probing" religious beliefs. It is not belief per se or the probing alone which is absolutely anathema. It is a compelled "profession" of belief which the First Amendment proscribes. That is the lesson of *Torcaso* and the sense of all that Justice Jackson wrote in West Virginia State Bd. of Educ. v. Barnette. But, Brennan's concept of "profession" was a more expansive concept. Ordination is an act but, in Brennan's assessment, an act expressive of intense belief and, when penalized by exclusion from political office, it is belief itself which is burdened. Surely, intense belief, like strong speech, is entitled to the same First Amendment protection as bland beliefs and weak words. The difference between intense belief and strong speech—and we exalt one aspect of Free Exercise above Free Speech when we state it—is that intense belief is absolute while strong speech does not permit one to scream "fire" in a crowded theatre, Schenck v. United States, supra, 249 U.S. at 52, nor permit what Chaplinsky v. New Hampshire, 315 U.S. 568 (1942), categorized as fighting words.

There are, for certain, limitations upon the Brennan concept of belief. He surely would agree with Chief Justice Waite's observation, in Reynolds v. United States, that it is not beyond the power of civil government to prevent a wife from burning herself "upon the funeral pile of her husband", however much her religious belief might tell her it is her religious duty to do so. Justice Brennan did suggest, however, that there are religious activities, beyond ordination, beyond priesthood, the ministry or the rabbinate, or the professed orders of any other church, which may instance symbolic and intense manifestations of belief. We may wonder, then, where the line is to be drawn between belief and conduct. We may wonder what other religiously rooted activities may be said to be so intimately identified with belief as to require the absolute protection found in the Constitutional command of freedom to believe.

In *McDaniel*, Justice Brennan wrote, of course, only of those disqualified by the Tennessee statute, ministers and priests. But, even in that context the question of where belief ends and conduct begins was not resolved. Chief Justice Burger wrote for four; Brennan for two, perhaps three, if we count in his favor Stewart's separate concurring notation, "As did Maryland in Torcaso, Tennessee has penalized an individual for his religious status —for what he is and believes in—rather than for any particular act generally deemed harmful to society"; Justice White invalidated the Tennessee statute on Equal Protection grounds, and Mr. Justice Blackmun did not participate in the consideration or decision of the case.

§ 3.02   Free Exercise—Establishment Tensions

Torcaso v. Watkins was one of those rather infrequent cases wherein the Establishment Clause and Free Exercise Clause operated in concert to invalidate a state statute. More often the Court has detected tensions in the First Amendment's Religion Clauses. Chief Justice Burger wrote in Walz v. Tax Comm'n., "The Court has struggled to find a neutral course between the two Religion Clauses, both of which are cast in absolute terms, and either of which, if expanded to a logical extreme, would tend to clash with the other." Long before *Walz*, Mr. Justice Black noted a tension of sorts. In *Everson* he appended to his Establishment Clause strictures the warning that the state "cannot hamper its citizens in the free exercise of their own religion" and, consequently, it cannot exclude individuals "because of their faith or lack of it" from receiving the benefit of public welfare legislation. How are those tensions, or seeming tensions, to be relaxed, or, when direct conflicts between the Free Exercise Clause and the Establishment Clause are found to exist, how are they to be resolved? It would be rather simplistic to suggest that the Establishment Clause by its terms is absolute "respecting an establishment of religion", while the Free Exercise proscription is directed at government prohibition, and not government protection, of religious liberty. For, it is obvious from what we have already seen of the Court's cases, that the

[287]

Free Exercise Clause has not acquired an invariable predominance over antiestablishment values.

Nine years before *Braunfeld*, Zorach v. Clauson approved a state program which released children from their public school regime to enable them to receive out-of-school religious training. There was an obvious conflict between the two Religion Clauses. *McCollum* had already condemned an in-school released time program, and both programs, that in *Zorach* and that in *McCollum*, were religiously inspired and each had the non-secular effect of promoting religious indoctrination. In *Zorach*, however, Mr. Justice Douglas was more conscious of religious liberty. He wrote an "accommodation" thesis, religious accommodation. But, whatever we may call it, *Zorach*'s holding was rooted in the Free Exercise Clause. *Zorach* "protected" the free exercise of religion without imposing any burden on any other individual's religious liberty. And it gave preference to Free Exercise accommodations over overly strict applications of the Establishment Clause. Douglas navigated the "neutral" course, which *Walz* espoused, between the two Religion Clauses.

The "wiser solution", which Warren proposed in Braunfeld v. Brown and which *Arlan's Department Store* casually affirmed, was as reasonable and as Constitutionally inoffensive as the release of children from a public school session one day a week so that they might receive religious training. A Sabbatarian exemption from Sunday Closing laws, though religiously motivated, simply served to unburden non-Sunday observers of the economic disadvantages which Sunday laws imposed upon the free exercise of their religion. Warren's "wiser solution" was an embodiment of *Zorach*'s accommodation doctrine. And it, too, was rooted in the Free Exercise Clause.

Nothing written in *Walz* or in *Zorach*, however, and nothing in Warren's "wiser solution", can be taken to mean that the limits of permissible state accommodations for religion are co-extensive with the noninterference mandated by the Free Exercise Clause. But, when are confronted by chaplains in the armed forces, Congressional chaplains, and chaplains in state and federal prisons, we are face to face with the ultimate confrontation. For, in the creation of chaplaincies government is subsidizing religion itself—with an evident affront to *Everson*'s dictate that no tax in any amount can be levied "to support any religious activities or institutions, whatever they may be called, or whatever form they may adopt to teach or practice religion."

On the several occasions when the Court, or an individual Justice, has paused to write in dicta of military and prison chaplains it has done so in terms highly protective of the Free Exercise of

Religion.   Concurring in Abington School Dist. v. Schempp, Justice Brennan wrote,

> There are certain practices, conceivably violative of the Establishment Clause, the striking down of which might seriously interfere with certain religious liberties also protected by the First Amendment. Provisions for churches and chaplains at military establishments for those in the armed services may afford one such example. The like provision by state and federal governments for chaplains in penal institutions may afford another example. It is argued that such provisions may be assumed to contravene the Establishment Clause, yet be sustained on constitutional grounds as necessary to secure to the members of the Armed Forces and prisoners those rights of worship guaranteed under the Free Exercise Clause. Since government has deprived such persons of the opportunity to practice their faith at places of their choice, the argument runs, government may, in order to avoid infringing the free exercise guarantees, provide substitutes where it requires such persons to be. 374 U.S. at 296–298.

In a similar vein Justice Stewart wrote in his *Schempp* dissent,

> [W]hile in many contexts the Establishment Clause and the Free Exercise Clause fully complement each other, there are areas in

which a doctrinaire reading of the Establishment Clause leads to irreconcilable conflict with the Free Exercise Clause.

A single obvious example should suffice to make the point. Spending federal funds to employ chaplains for the armed forces might be said to violate the Establishment Clause. Yet a lonely soldier stationed at some faraway outpost could surely complain that a government which did *not* provide him the opportunity for pastoral guidance was affirmatively prohibiting the free exercise of his religion. 374 U.S. at 309.

All federal penitentiaries and reformatories provide chapels and chaplains, clergymen in clerical garb, to give religious instruction and to conduct religious services for inmates, and chaplain salaries are paid by the federal government. In Cruz v. Beto, 405 U.S. 319 (1972), the Court implicitly approved far more than the payment of chaplain salaries. The complaint of a Texas state prison inmate alleged that "Texas encourages inmates to participate in other religious programs, providing at state expense chaplains of the Catholic, Jewish and Protestant faiths; providing also at state expense copies of the Jewish and Christian Bibles and conducting weekly Sunday school classes and religious services." Plaintiff, a Buddhist complained that equal religious facilities and services were not provided for him and members of his faith. The Court expressed no concern at all about the state's subsidization of religion. It implicitly accepted its Constitutionality. For, it remanded to the District Court for a hearing only on petitioner's claim of discrimination.

Cruz v. Beto presented a direct conflict, an one-on-one contest, between the Free Exercise Clause and the Establishment Clause. Each of the Religion Clauses was expanded to its drily logical extreme and the religious freedom of prisoners prevailed over *Everson*'s explicit dictate that no tax in any amount shall be levied to support any religious activities. The most that can be said of Cruz v. Beto's exaltation of religious liberty, however, is that it sanctioned the funding of prison chaplains and prison chapels because it was reasonably necessary to permit those in custody to practice their religion, even though the expenditure of government funds for the advancement of religion might be Constitutionally barred in another setting. The elementary and secondary parochial schools present the other setting.

In the private elementary and secondary school setting, sectarian and non-sectarian, one aspect of liberty was fiirmly established in 1925 in Pierce v. Society of Sisters, supra. *Pierce* struck down an Oregon statute which mandated that all children in that state attend, through primary and secondary grades, only public schools. *Pierce* sustained the right of the parent to send his or her child to a parochial school, the right to dictate the religious education of the child. Mr. Justice McReynolds wrote, "[t]he fundamental theory of liberty upon which all governments in this Union repose excludes any general power of the State to standardize its children by forcing them to accept instruction from public teachers only. The child is not the mere creature of the State; those who nurture him and direct his destiny have the right, coupled with the high duty, to recognize and prepare him for additional obligations." 268 U.S. at 535.

Pierce was not a First Amendment decision. It antedated the Court's absorption of the Religion Clauses into the Fourteenth Amendment's Due Process Clause. But, the parental right was classified as a fundamental First Amendment right in Griswold v. Connecticut, supra, 381 U.S. at 482, 483. And in *Yoder*, Chief Justice Burger, reaffirming *Pierce*, stated that the fundamental right of parents to guide the religious future and education of their children "is now established beyond doubt as an enduring American tradition."

The existence of that right, however fundamental and enduring it may be, does not mean that its exercise must be or may be financed by the state. The state is no more required to subsidize parents who send their children to parochial schools than it is "to pay the bus fares of indigent travelers" who exercise their fundamental right to travel interstate. See Maher v. Roe, 432 U.S. 464, 474–475, n.8 (1977). The state may, with Constitutional impunity, choose to pay the bus fares of indigent interstate travelers. But, even the payment of bus fares of those who travel to a sectarian parochial school raises, as *Everson's* 5–4 decision made evident, a serious Establishment problem. And, as *Nyquist* held, modest tuition reimbursements or tax credits for impoverished parents who choose to send their children to religious schools, as is their parental and Free Exercise-allied right, are impermissible. Free Exercise and Establishment Clause tensions do exist. But, in the post-*Lemon I* era of parochial school cases the Court has, as we have already seen, very strictly limited the very few areas of permissible state aid for children, and the parents of children, who attend church-related elementary and secondary schools.

In those post-*Lemon I* cases a majority of the Court evidently found the prohibitions of the Establishment Clause so compelling that there was little need to assess potential Free Exercise claims. There is no question that in the majority's view the Establishment Clause, in that context, took predominance over the Free Exercise guarantees. Six Justices of the present Court have now established themselves as strict antiestablishment disciplinarians in church-related elementary and secondary schools cases. Justice White, most certainly, and Chief Justice Burger and Justice Rehnquist have been the most frequent dissenters.

Justice White and Justice Rehnquist have consistently and persistently espoused educational equality for all children, whether in private or in public schools. And Justice White, in particular, has repeatedly noted the redundancy in the excessive entanglement part of the tripartite test of Establishment, and has constantly challenged, as excessive, the Court's application of the tripartite test in the parochial school cases. On the whole Justice Rehnquist has subscribed to the White philosophy, but he has also sensed Free Exercise Clause aberrations in the majority's application of the Establishment Clause. So, too, has Chief Justice Burger. Each noted his concern in Meek v. Pittenger.

"The Court apparently believes," Rehnquist wrote, "that the Establishment Clause of the First Amendment not only mandates religious neutrality on the part of government but also requires that this Court go further and throw its weight on the side of those who believe that our society as a whole should be a purely secular one." Chief Justice Burger's censure was a little more specific and perhaps a little more severe. "One can only hope," he said, "that at some future date the Court will come to a more enlightened and tolerant view of the First Amendment's guarantee of free exercise of religion, thus eliminating the denial of equal protection to children in church-sponsored schools, and take a more realistic view that carefully limited aid to children is not a step toward establishing a state religion—at least while this Court sits."

There is no doubt that the six prevailing Justices of the present Court have reserved *Everson*'s sternest Establishment Clause strictures for the elementary and secondary parochial schools. Given the complete dominance of the Establishment Clause over the Free Exercise values in those cases, it will be a long night's journey into day for the Chief Justice to find the enlightenment he seeks. That he will see the day in a parochial school case, the auguries are not auspicious—certainly not while this Court sits.

INDEX

References are to Pages

INDEX

[*298*]

INDEX

INDEX

†